THE REDEEMER AND THE DRAGON

The Epic Of Three Kingdoms

'Dipo Toby Alakija

ISBN: 978-978-36348-3-1
ISBN: 978-36348-3-6

Printed in United States
Published by the publishing house of

CALVARY ROCK RESOURCES

19, Ajina Street, Ikenne Remo,
Ogun State,
Nigeria.

36, Thomson road
Gorton
Manchester
M18 7QQ
United Kingdom

270 Madison Avenue
Suite 1500, New York, NY 10016
United States

www.calvaryrock.org

Dedication

This book is dedicated to heroes of faith in the Bible and in this generation. It is also dedicated to my wife, Omolade Martha Alakija for standing by my side in struggles and in battles.

THE REDEEMER AND THE DRAGON

There is a kingdom of Eternity,
Which has no beginning and no end.
Another kingdom was made to come,
Which is made up of fire and brimstone.
Another kingdom was created for man
But man lost the dominion to evil one.

These kingdoms are as real as life
But what is not real to most people
Is the battle every man must fight
Because the evil one knows how to strike
Without showing any form of appearance
Man is lost in all the battlefields of life.

Jesus Christ came to fight all our battles
He does not look real to so many people
That is why they treat Him with levity
But He is as real as the dates we are born
He delivers as many as believe in His name
And leads them to the kingdom of Eternity.

CHAPTER ONE

Brethren is one of the giants that are mandated to look after followers of The Redeemer called Believers. Among other things, the giant has the responsibilities to groom and train Believers into warriors that would effectively combat their immortal enemies in the battlefield called The Spirit.

Other giant warriors of The Redeemer include Faithful, Blessed, Redeemed, Justified, Sanctified, Beloved and a host of others. So many things characterize these giant warriors, which make it possible for them to be victorious in nearly every battle, including the ones in The Spirit, The Flesh and The Mind. These giants are united by the Spirit of The Redeemer called Comforter. Through Comforter, giants are able to possess and also help other Believers to possess the armies of Comforter called Love, Joy, Peace, Longsuffering Gentleness, Goodness, Faith, Meekness, Temperance and a host of others.

Just as there are levels of powers and ranks among the soldiers of the enemy of the people called Dragon, there are also stages of maturity among Believers. The stages are basically three. Stage one is the birth into the family of The Redeemer while stage two is the babes, which is the beginning of maturity. The third stage is adulthood, which is the matured stage. Actually, as long as all Believers are not yet with The Redeemer in the place called Eternity, they need to grow in maturity in the kingdom of man called the earth or world.

The growths of all Believers depend on what they take spiritually. Hence if they constantly feed on the food called The Word and obey the instructions of The Redeemer, they grow faster. The more they feed on The Word, the more strength they gather. If, however, at any point, they do not feed on The Word, they become starved. Just as all living things can die through starvation, Believers too can die if they are starved of The Word or if they do not follow the instructions of The

Redeemer, no matter their levels.

Other ways Believers grow or die is through the kind of people they mix up with. As people have many ways of influencing one another everywhere, Believers are mandated by The Redeemer to always gather for meetings at places called Fellowship, where they can feed on The Word and get strengths for the battles, which always engage them through out their lives. He even gives them some rules to follow. Three of the rules are: they must love one another, they must be united and they must encourage one another with The Word.

Before the spread of Believers all over the world, shortly after the Redeemer has gone to Eternity to prepare mansions for his people, there was strict adherence to the rules. In fact, it is in the history of Believers that they did things in common. This unity gave them so much strengths that Dragon and his soldiers are seriously threatened. They did all they could to scatter them, using people who were not Believers to persecute them. Instead of achieving his aim to ambush and destroy them, however, the enemies only made them to increase and spread to every nook and cranny of the world.

As time went by, Dragon begins to apply various methods, using so many instruments, weapons of war and even people to make Believers break the rules, especially the golden ones which is to constantly feed on The Word like food and follow the instructions of The Redeemer.

The organization of the armies of Dragon is so complex that nobody except The Redeemer understands it. Through Comforter who always explains it through The Word, however, the giants are able to get pictures of the organization. The Giants who has teaching grace sometimes explain it to other Believers in the way a normal person can understand it.

There are three broad levels of enemies of Believers. All Believers must battle and defeat all the enemies in these levels before they become giants. Of course, these giants always get the attention of Dragon. If any giant gets his attention, he is bound to face more intense battles and temptations that are often orchestrated by a host of Wickedness.

The first level is called Principalities. The enemies in this group are the ones New Birth or Babe Believers always face in the battlefield of The Flesh. The Word of The Redeemer explains that only by walking in The Spirit can anyone overcome everyone of them. If they are engaged in The Flesh, the smallest of these enemies is big enough to bring down even a giant Believer.

The enemies in this group includes warriors like Adultery,

Fornication, Uncleanness, Lasciviousness, Idolatry, Witchcraft, Hatred, Variance, Emulations, Wrath, Strife, Seditions, Heresies, Envyings, Murders, Drunkenness, Revellings and a host of others.

These enemies are tough to overcome for Believers in the stage of new birth but if they give Comforter the chance to operate in their lives, they can easily take the battle from The Flesh into The Spirit where they can easily get victories.

Once that they are able to get victories over Principalities, the Babe Believers grow into the next stage called Young Believers. The Young Believers are faced with another group of enemies called Powers, which also operate in The Flesh although they also operated in the two other battlefields called The Mind and The Spirit.

The enemies in the group of Powers are broadly sub-divided into three called Lust Of The Flesh, Lust Of The Eyes and The Pride Of Life. These enemies often use the human senses of perceptions as means of bringing Young Believers down. These senses include the use of the eyes, the nose, the ears, the mouth and the body. The things in the world are made so glamorous and attractive to their eyes that they crave for them. It is after they possess them that they realize that they have lost the citizenship of Eternity called Salvation. More often than not, Young Believers that fall do not realize they have lost their Salvation until it is too late - the time they depart from the world. It is when they get to Eternity that they would be denied access to the Kingdom of The Father. Then they would be cast into Eternal Doom kingdom of the Dragon, which is a lake of fire and brimstone.

Because these enemies are so powerful, subtle and quite invisible, they are not easy to detect and overcome. Each of them has so many ways of taking stronghold of human body and keeps it under the control of Dragon. Comforter who is part of The Redeemer is the only one who empowers all levels of Believers to overcome all the enemies if they give Him room to operate in their lives.

The main reason Believers lose out to those enemies is that they do not allow Comforter full control of their lives. Some Believers grieve Him so much that He has to leave them alone. Of course, once the Believers are on their own, they stand no chance to overcome even the smallest of their enemies. If, however, Comforter is given full control in their lives, Believers find it easy to overcome the combined forces of these powerful enemies.

Every Believer who is able to overcome the enemies at the second level is empowered to face and battle with the enemies in the third stage called Rulers of Darkness.

The Rulers of Darkness are not ordinary enemies of Believers. They are actually members of decision making council of Eternal Doom, which is headed by Dragon. Because there are always numerous matters to debate and decide on, The Rulers of Darkness never discuss any matter or problem which either Principalities or Powers can handle. They discuss special cases, relating to Believers that are in the level of giants of The Redeemer.

The giants of The Redeemer are the Believers who have graduated from all the other stages of Believers into soldiers that are more than conquerors. Most Believers never make it to the level of giants before they are taken to Eternal Bliss. They always battle with the enemies in levels one and two for years before The Redeemer takes them out of kingdom of man. Only those who had been specially trained by The Redeemer have what it is takes to face The Rulers of Darkness. In fact a lot of giants who were not careful enough had been captured and destroyed by the enemies in this level. They have also reduced so many others giants who are once more than conquerors into meat for small enemies in level one or two to devour.

When a giant falls, many Believers at the lower levels usually fall with him. That is one of the main reason The Rulers of Darkness concentrate their efforts on giants. The enemies have so many ways of reducing giants into eat but before the enemies know how to tackle him, they would first study his strengths and weaknesses. Naturally, every Believer has his weak points but no matter how weak, if Comforter is given the full control and he adheres to every instruction of The Redeemer, his constant victories are assured.

Fighting The Rulers of Darkness is very tough for all Believers because these enemies never give up on anyone of them nor give them any breathing space. Believers have to be careful about so many things, including money, sex and pride. These three things, as little weapons as they seem are too deadly for any Believer to get involved in, no matter his or her level. Even then, the deadliest among these weapons is pride. Pride has a way of making Believer un-teachable or unrepentant. Once a Believer is overcome with pride, his total destruction in lake of fire in Eternal Doom is inevitable. Pride can make all levels of Believers to reject correction. Once correction is rejected, a Believer moves from one error right into another until he ends up in the camp of his enemies who are ready to destroy him in The Flesh and The Spirit.

The Redeemer knows how deadly pride is. So he tells all Believers to be clothed with a garment of virtue called Humility. Once a

Believer is clothed with Humility, it becomes easy for him to learn and accept correction once he is going wrong. Even then, pride makes it difficult for many Believers, especially at the base level to see Humility as a garment of virtue. In fact, he makes them see it as humiliation or embarrassment. Hence, wherever pride is operating, everything in the life of a Believer goes wrong and tends to go the way of destruction.

Brethren who is among the giants that are mandated by The Redeemer to look after some Believers is fervent, strong and so skillful that he is almost perfect. He is a constant source of headaches to The Rulers Of Darkness. He has made lots of enemies for Dragon by building other Believers into warriors of The Redeemer. The warriors in turn also create more enemies for soldiers of Dragon to content with. What actually makes Brethren a dangerous giant is not only in his ability to convert non-Believers into Believers or train Believers to become conquerors, but also lies in his garment of virtue of humility he always put on. This makes it easy for him to immediately take correction from others whenever he goes wrong. Unlike some other giants who often times feel embarrassed or humiliated whenever they are rebuked openly when they go wrong, Brethren always admits faults as his even if sometimes they are not. In the course of trying to get him down, however, the enemies discover that he has high sexual urge. They set a beautiful spinster called Sister Flirt to get him down through sex but, because he constantly confesses his weakness to Comforter, he is able to overcome the temptation through his wife who made herself available on their matrimonial bed.

Desperate to get him down through sex, the enemies used Flirt to fall deeply in love with Brethren. She secretly nurses the feelings of love though she knows that he is married. She pretends to be in need of his wise counsel just to have a conversation with him. Whenever they are together in the counseling room, she always pictures him on the bed with her, playing love together. Of course, she does not always concentrate on what he is sharing with her in The Word. She was always thinking of how she would succeed in making him love her in return.

CHAPTER TWO

Sister Flirt is in the congregation as Brethren feeds the people with The Word in the meeting of Believers at the Fellowship. The meeting is usually attended by mixed multitudes of different levels of Believers and non-Believers. People of different walks of life are duly represented there. The people that are present at the Fellowship include those who are falling, standing and fighting in the battle against armies of the Dragon. So Brethren, knowing that the only way to help them stand firm and keep them strong is to feed them with the undiluted Word. Through The Word that is made available by The Redeemer, giant Brethren can heal the sick, comfort the uncomfortable, give hope to the hopeless, encourage those who are discouraged and enrich those who are poor.

He says, reading from The Word called the Bible, 'The Word in the book of Jeremiah Chapter nine verses twenty-three and twenty-four says. "Thus says the LORD, Let not the wise man glory in his wisdom, neither let the mighty man glory in his might, let not the rich man glory in his riches: But let him that glories glory in this, that he understands and knows me, that I am the LORD Who exercises loving kindness, judgment, and righteousness, in the earth: for in these things I delight, says the LORD." '

Brethren looks round at the people, feeling a little concerned about the condition of most of them. He can perceive what they are going through on the battlefields in The Mind, The Flesh and The Spirit. Many of them are wounded even though they are good at concealing their wounds. He knows that a lot of them are going through needless pains because they are ignorance of their enemies that are fighting them every time. Many of them are already dead in The Spirit, waiting to be buried at Eternal Doom without even knowing it. However, he knows how to bring back to life those who are dead in all the battlefields, heal the wounded and the broken hearted with The

8

Word of the Redeemer. If they develop the appetite to take and use The Word of the Redeemer as meat in Tho Spirit, water in The Mind and medicine in The Flesh; they would all be delivered from their pains and sorrows. He has no power to bring back to the kingdom of man those who are already in Eternal Doom but he knows that with the appetite for The Word called Faith, there is nothing impossible for all Believers to do. So he sees it as his primary duty to feed the people with The Word and let Comforter to do the rest of the job.

'The topic we are treating today is: Don't let anything or anyone to mislead you,' Brethren continues feeding the people with The Word. 'The Word says that no one should glory in his wisdom because the Redeemer instructs us in the book of Proverb chapter 3 verse 5 that we should not lean our understanding. We must not also glory in our might because we are made to understand in the first book of Samuel chapter 2 verse 9 that The Redeemer will keep the feet of His saints, and the wicked shall be silent in darkness; for by strength shall no man prevail. Lastly, we must not glory in riches because it can be deceptive. We should only glory that we know The Redeemer and that He knows us. And He calls us by our names.

'People can be misled by wisdom of man, by might and riches of this world but the instruction is: do not let anything or anyone to mislead you.' He pauses for a while as he flips through pages of The Word.

'Read with me The Word in Romans chapter two verse eighteen to twenty-four. The passage says, "And know his will (that is the is will of The Redeemer), and approve the things that are excellent, being instructed out of the law, and are confident that you yourself are a guide to the blind, a light to those who are in darkness, an instructor of the foolish, a teacher of babes, having the form of knowledge and truth in the law. You, therefore, who teach another, do you not teach yourself? You who preach that a man should not steal, do you steal? You who say, do not commit adultery, do you not commit adultery? You who abhor idols, do you rob temples? You who make your boast in the law, do you dishonor the father through breaking this law? For "the name of the Father is blasphemed among non-Believers because of you" as it is written.'

He looks at the people at the Fellowship for a while before he says, 'I am sure the passage is clear enough but I still need to bring out a few things to your notice. Through this passage, I am able see two things. One of them is the way people mislead others. Secondly, you can also know when you're misled. Let's start with how people mislead others, going by the passage we just read.

'In verse twenty-three, we can infer that people can be misled by words of others. Words are powerful. So you have to be sure of the kinds of words you take. Just as truth can come in form of words, lies; deceptions and falsehood can also come in the form of words. A very good example is the case of our fore parents called Adam and Eve. When the Eternal Father who is in Eternity created this kingdom for man, he gave it to these parents to rule. He gave them also the law to follow. He made them understand that the day they break the law, they would begin to die.

'Now Dragon who has been kicked out of Eternity with his servants who are in all the classes of our enemies wanted to take over this kingdom by all means. Dragon went to Adam and Eve in the form of a friendly neighbour called Serpent and tricked them into breaking the law. He was able to persuade Eve through mere words. Through the same words, she was able to persuade her husband, Adam to also break this law. The moment they broke the law, they lost this kingdom to Dragon. Since that time, Dragon had been in charge of the kingdom of man, making life terrible for everybody, including you and me.

'Words are powerful enough. So be careful with whatever you believe. Do not accept anything that contradicts The Word, please! The reason is that it can cost you your life in Eternity.

'Still talking about The Word,' Brethren continues after a brief pause, 'Dragon now has lots of human servants that are spreading all over the kingdom, using the same old trick to dissuade people from the path of Eternal Bliss. These servants are so eloquent that if you are not deep rooted in The Word, you will be deceived and misled. Some of these servants appear like Believers while some appear as intellectuals that see our faith in the Redeemer as a form of brainwashing or mere religion that are characterized by those who want to make us monkeys or zombies out of us. They believe we have no sense of our own. So they make us appear like fools. Guess what! The Word says in Psalm one hundred and eleven verse ten that the fear of the Eternal Father is the beginning of wisdom and a good understand have all those who do his commandments.

'Dragon will no longer appear like serpents as he did to our fore parents. No, sir! He will not even appear in his true form because he knows we will recognize him easily. He will come to you as a Believer or even giant servant of the Redeemer if he knows you're a smart Believer. He will come to you as an entertainer if he knows you like being entertained. He will come to you as an academician if he knows you are a bookworm. He will blend to your taste or interest. If he knows you love sex, he will come to you as a handsome man or a beautiful lady that is in love with you. His ways and appearances had become so complex that you cannot afford to be negligent. Believe me, you cannot be too careful. So you must take The Word of the Redeemer as your daily meal otherwise Dragon will mislead you through falsehood and lies.

'The second way people are misled is through deeds as we can see it in verse twenty-two of chapter two of the book of Romans. In this case, we see someone whose words and deeds as Believers never match. He teaches people not to commit adultery but he is neck deep in it. He forgets what The Word says about the life of Believers reflecting what they believe in second Corinthians chapter three verse two, which says that all Believers have The Word written in their hearts and read by all men. But what do we have today? Many so-called Believers preach the truth but they never live by the truth. While their words lead some people to the right way, their deeds lead others astray. Such people are regarded as borrowed vessels which The Redeemer uses to teach people what is right but on the day decision would be taken about where to spend their eternity, He will tell the hypocrites, "depart from me, you worker of iniquities I don't know you," going by The Word in Matthew chapter seven verses twenty-one to twenty three.

'When people tell you anything in The Word, search by yourself and find out if it is true. If it is, hold it. If it is not, spit if out. When the life of anyone who calls himself a Believer does not match The Word, correct him with love. If he takes correction, you have saved him from destruction. If he does not take it, leave him alone but don't ever follow him to do the wrong thing.

'The third way people are misled is through the fruits or works of others. The redeemer says in Matthew chapter seven verses fifteen to twenty that we should be beware of false Believers, who come to us in sheep's clothing, but inwardly they are ravenous wolves. You will know them by their fruits. "Do men gather grapes from thorn bushes or figs from thistles? Even so, every good tree bears good fruit, but a bad tree bears bad fruit. A good tree cannot bear bad fruit, nor can a bad tree bear good fruit. Every tree that does not bear good fruit is cut down and thrown into the fire. Therefore by their fruits you will know them." '

He pauses for a while to take his breath before he continues, 'fruits can come in any form like works of your hands or attitudes. The trees in the passage represent different kinds of people we have in the entire kingdom of man. There are good and bad trees. The question is: how do you know a good tree, according to that passage? It is by their fruits. Likewise, we know a true Believer through his or her attitude or works. The Word says in James chapter two verse seventeen, "thus also faith by itself if it does not have works is dead." We also read in verses fifteen and sixteen of that passage, "if a brother or sister is naked and destitute of daily food, and one of you say to them, 'Depart in peace, be warmed and filled,' but you do not give the things which are needed for the body, what does it profit?" We can see it clearly that our works or fruits as good trees. Many Believers, instead of giving what their brothers need, they would offer only prayers even though they are in the position to be of help. That kind of attitude actually produces a bad fruit called hypocrisy.

'How can people be misled by works or fruits of others? This is a very interesting question. There are some works or fruits that seem so good like the one Dragon showed to Eve when he was about to mislead or deceive her. Let's study the case in the book of Genesis chapter three, starting from verse two, it reads like this: "And the woman (that's Eve) said to the serpent (that's Dragon), we may eat the fruit of the trees of the garden, but of the fruit of the tree which is in the midst of the garden, God has said, 'you shall not eat it, nor shall you touch it, lest you die.' " For the sake of time, let's skip the rest of the verses and study verse six there. The place says, "So when the woman saw that the tree was good for food, that it was pleasant to the eyes, and a tree desirable to make one wise, she took the fruit and ate...." This is where I'm going. All the things Eternal Father created are good but, the moment He says that you must not touch a particular thing, it becomes bad for you to touch. Yes, it was the fruit that makes man wise. That may seem like a proof to you that it is good. It is, however, bad for Adam or Eve to eat because it is Eternal Father, the source of their lives that made it a law for them not to eat it.

'Don't smell, let alone to eat it! Don't touch it, let alone to smell it. Don't go near it, let alone to look at it. The breaking of this golden rule is what brings about the fall of man, making him to lose the kingdom to Dragon. Man who is supposed to be the king in his kingdom becomes slave of the new king which is Dragon. Since that time up till now, man finds himself desiring what God hates. He gets involved in things that can easily destroy him. In other words, by breaking be law, he lost the control of himself and the control of his kingdom to Dragon, his great enemy. I want you to note here that the battle in this kingdom is not the battle between man and man, not between wife and husband, not between children and parents and not between families and families. The truth is: it is Dragon that fights Eternal Father because of man, whom He loves so much that He sent His Eternal Son, the Redeemer to redeem and fight for man. Like I once shared with you, Dragon is too strong for anyone to handle. He has more than enough good reasons to fight Eternal Father over man. We find ourselves in crossfire even before we were born. Up till now, this enemy is fighting and enslaving so many people through the use of everything, including what Eternal Father has given to everybody to enjoy in this kingdom. He uses various levels of armies and different tricks with visible and invisible weapons that vary from time to time, from generations to generations to engage everybody, including children in the battle. He is using things that seem very beautiful and pleasant to lure Believers from the Redeemer. Sex is wonderful and enjoyable if it is within the confine of marriage but I tell you if you engage in it outside your marriage, you a dead person. Now death is in two ways. What man considers as death is not really death but sleep, going by what The Word says in First Thessalonians Chapter 4 Verse 14. Since man is made up of body, spirit and soul, there are three ways a person can cease to live. One of them is to be transformed or transported from the body which is physical to Eternity either in Eternal Bliss where The Redeemer is seated at the right Hand of The Eternal Father or in Eternal Doom, where Dragon and his messengers reign. Death, therefore, is not a substantive or an objective thing. Death is not the opposite of life but the absence of life. Real death is both spiritual and eternal. Spiritual death is the condition of a person who does not have in his life The Redeemer who happens to be the way to Eternal Bliss, the truth we read in The Word and the life in the lives of all Believers. Thus anyone who is not a Believer is spiritually dead! If he remains in that condition until he goes out of the kingdom of man, he will go right straight to Eternal Doom which, is according to The Word in Revelation Chapter 21 Verse 8, second death - the eternal death in the lake that burns with fire and brimstone.' He pauses to look round at the engrossed congregation. 'That's scary, isn't? I tell you it is much scarier than that.

'The other thing Dragon uses to get people to Eternal Doom is money. Money is a good thing to have if the Redeemer says it is good for you but if you attach your love to it, evil and eternal death is around your corner. To occupy the position of influence is good also, if the Redeemer places you there but if you are the one that place yourself there or you let your status in life get into your head, pride will set you on the wrong path which is the path of eternal death.

However, no matter the state of your life in The Spirit whether you are dead, dying or wounded, I can assure that the Redeemer will restore you today if you go to Him in The Spirit. He is always waiting for everybody to come and meet Him there through the vehicle called Prayer. If you are humble enough to go to Him, He will bring you back to life if you are dead. He will give you the power to bind and to lose. He will give you the power to destroy the works of the enemies even if you a babe Believer because He knows that no one can overcome Dragon on his own. He will give you the power to recover what you have lost and also the power to bring back back to life others who are dead in The Spirit and The Mind. That's the confidence we have as we sing:

Dry bones shall rise again!
Dry bones shall rise again…
Lord, our Father is able
To do all things…
He is more than able
To do all things…

CHAPTER THREE

Dragon is having the usual meeting with Rulers of darkness who are his council members. Although this council is the highest in authority in kingdom of man and darkness, not much is known about them. In fact, they prefer to appear like creatures that exist only in imaginations. This form of appearance is essential to conceal their operations. Apart from The Word which exposes them and their activities, there is no other way anyone could ever perceive or imagine their existence. This tactic proves to be very effective as the people, including Believers ignorantly walk into the trap that are set for them by all the levels of their enemies. This council is the one that often sets trap for Giant Believers or conquerors. If they have to go to the Father in Eternity to get permission to bring any giant down, Dragon always goes there by himself.

Among the Rulers of Darkness are some highly dangerous enemies called Ignorance of The Word, Disunity, Arrogance, Prayerlessness, Compromise, Indiscipline, Disobedience and a large host of others. One of the dangerous characteristics of each of these enemies is that they look so mild, gentle or subtle. It is very hard to explain their complexities and gauge their strengths. Most, if not all of these rulers, command large armies who are either in the category of Principalities or Powers. Ignorance has in his army warriors like Heresies, False Doctrines, Human knowledge among so many others. Disunity has in his own army Variance, Wrath, Hatred, Jealousy, Envy and Insecurities who can transform into any other soldiers, including the ones that operate as Ignorance and Arrogance. Arrogance has Pride, Holier-Than-Thou Attitude, Judgmental Spirit, Un-teachable Spirit, Haughty Spirit, Rebellion and a host of others in his army. Prayerlessness is one hell of a ruler who has what it takes to use any of the warriors to fight against the people either in The Spirit or The Flesh or The Mind. Once Prayerlessness strike a giant, the

Believer takes a nose dive into destruction. Compromise commands nearly all the warriors that can fight in The Flesh and The Mind. Such warriors include Sex, Vanity, Love Of Money, Uncleanness, Abominations, Hypocrisy, Lust of the Eyes, Lust of The Flesh and Pride of life. Indiscipline is another terrifying ruler that can use any warriors that can fight the people in all the battlefields, including The Spirit. Disobedience is a small and mild looking ruler that can open ways for even the smallest of the warriors to attack and destroy the people. He can empower a small warrior like Carelessness to bring down a giant Believer. He has in his team Rebellion, Human Wisdom, Head Knowledge and Unbelief who is good at fighting all Believers and non-Believers. Whenever any ruler of darkness wants to bring down a giant, Disobedience will first attempt to disarm him of The Word which serves as the sword with which he fights. Then Ignorance would begin to undo what The Word has done in his life. He will take all his armor of war, one after the other. Even then, he may still have some strength until Comforter is grieved and allowed to leave the giant. The smallest of the warrior can finish him up at that stage. Most Believers, especially giants do not fall suddenly but gradually. In fact The Word constantly warns every Believer that those who think they stand should take heed, least they fall. More emphatically, Comforter continues to stress the fact that it is easier to fall than to stand. The higher the level of a Believer, the harder it is to rise again if he or she falls. Again, because a lot of people normally fall through the fall of a giant, Dragon concentrates the efforts of his council members who work with him as a host of wickedness on the fall of giant Believers. He prefers to keep fallen giants alive in the kingdom of man after killing them in The Spirit and The Mind so that he can use them to bring other Believers down. Since this battle strategy proves to be very effective, he does not border himself about non-Believers, babes or even matured Believers. Instead of giving any of them his attention, he assigns Principalities and Powers to handle them.

Dragon is feeling worried lately because of the activities of some giant Believers like Brethren who are wrecking havoc into his kingdom, exposing his operations and creating more enemies for him through sound teachings of The Word. If the giants have limited it at that, it would have been more tolerable to some extent. Brethren in particular knows how to use The Word with the backing of Comforter to wake up sleeping giants, bringing back to life Believers that are dead in The Spirit and The Mind. He seems too strong for them to handle. So they need to hold meetings and find way - any way - to

16

tackle him before he grows completely out of hand.

'What are you doing about the case of Brethren and other giants that are threatening our kingdoms?' Dragon asks, going straight to the point without beating about the bush. He does not have a definite form of appearance. He can appear like a monster, a serpent, a gentleman and even a servant on the Redeemer, depending on the nature of his operation or whom he wants to deal with. Because he is addressing his council members who all in attendance at the meeting in their true forms, Dragon is in the appearance of hideous looking monster with horns on both sides of his head.

There is no response as Dragon looks round at them.

'I'll take that as admission that you've all failed,' he says to them.

'No, my lord,' Ignorance is the first to come up with a defense. 'You know, my lord, that it is very hard if not impossible for me to operate where The Word of the Redeemer is shared and applied. Brethren is always feeding on The Word. That is the main reason I find it hard to get close to him, let alone to bring him down.'

Dragon looks at the rest, expecting their responses. Arrogance shrugs indifferently and says, 'well, master, Brethren is always cloth with garment of Humility. So it is hard, if not impossible to defeat him. If only I can get a way to tear the garment of humility, I won't have problem reducing him into meat for other warriors to devour. But Comforter is always with him, reminding him of The Word that exposes me and co-warriors like Pride and Boasting as destroyers. Brethren is quite insulated against our attack though we are always looking for opportunities to strike him down.'

Prayerlessness clears his throat before he says, 'my lord, Comforter is my major problem in dealing with Brethren and other giants that are giving us problems. Each time I weaken them, Comforter will give them strength again. In fact, he will give them more powers to shell us. It's like each time I try to get him down, he gets more power from Comforter to attack us. So I have to stay away from for a while because I don't want to add more to the problem on ground.'

Compromise hesitates for a while before he says, 'I've tried several times to use warriors like Vanity, Root of All Evil, Sex Appeal, Uncleanness and so many others like that but the problem still boils on the fact that these giants have superior weapons and Comforter, the Supreme Being on their side. I always try to drive away Comforter and take The Word from them through the use of these warriors. Right now, we are trying to use a beautiful lady called Sister Flirt in the congregation of Brethren. She is a babe Believer, if not a dead one but she poses as a matured Believer. She is constantly battling with one of our warriors in the class of Principalities called Masturbation. I use the warrior called Deception to convince her that she is still a very sound and matured Believer. With the two warriors working on her, Fornication and Adultery are already well informed of the missions against giant Brethren. Deception, Masturbation and Fornication will use her to get Brethren down. Even though we have gone far in this plan, we still expect big problem in getting Brethren down through Sister Flirt. The reason is that his wife is making up for his sexual urge, which is the route we hope to get at him. But, having gone this far, there is no going back. We therefore invited Carelessness to handle Brethren's wife.'

Dragon smiles for the first time, an indication that he was impressed by the report of activities of Compromise so far.

He looks at Indiscipline and nods at him, expecting him to give his own report.

'My lord,' Indiscipline says, 'I wouldn't say I have achieved anything so write home about. The power of the giant would have been greater than this if not for the fact that I am able to reduce his power.'

'How?' Dragon sounds irritated. With the outright failure on the part of most of the council members, he really does not expect anyone to bluff about reducing the power of some major threats.

'Well, my lord,' indiscipline say softly. 'I... am... I am able to reduce his power through lack of self-denial of food that can increase his strength.'

'Apparently,' Dragon says, looking more irritated, 'you have reduced nothing because he is able to make up in other areas. You probably don't know the giant we are talking about here. He has what it takes to crush us without sweat, going by what he has done so far.'

'I'm sorry, my lord,' Indiscipline says. 'I've not done enough.'

Disobedience says after a brief silence, 'the challenge I'm having with the giants is about the same with others. Comforter assigns some soldiers like Love, Joy, Peace, Goodness, Faithfulness, Gentleness, Self-control and a host of others to Believers that are frustrating our efforts.

'The most power of these soldiers is Love who actually brought down The Redeemer to redeem the people from us. If we cause any major havoc in the kingdom of man, Love alone can undo it. If we kill anyone in The Spirit or The Mind, Love is powerful enough to bring him

18

back to life. No matter the number of people on the path of Eternal Doom, Love can still lead them to the path of Eternal Bliss.' He pauses for a while, looking at Dragon. 'My lord, I am sure I am telling you what you already know.'

The rest looks at Dragon, expecting him to confirm if he is saying the truth.

Instead of saying a word, Dragon only looks frustrated. This, of course, confirms that Disobedience is telling the truth.

'What makes Love so powerful is because he is actually the central part of Eternal Father. Other parts of Eternal Father that are working against us are Mercy, Compassion and Favour....'

'That's enough!' Dragon says suddenly. 'We've not come here to discuss that. We've got no time to talk about the strengths of our enemies. We have to find ways to bring each and every one of them down.' He looks at Disunity who is silent, waiting for the opportunity to address the council. 'You've not given us your reports, Disunity. Let's have it now. I can do with some good reports.'

'My lord,' Disunity says. 'If you check my records you'll note that I have brought down many giants. I used the usual method of making them to fight one another with the same weapon they are supposed to use against us.'

'We all know that,' Dragon says impatiently, 'You must understand that we won't get anywhere if we talk about our achievements. So let's talk about our failures and how we can turn them into successes.'

Disunity hesitates for a while before he says, 'my lord. What Disobedience said is from experience, which we have to learn in a hard way. We have to admit that there are some giants that are too dangerous for us to contend with.'

'I disagree!' Arrogance says.

Dragon smiles. He seems to find something that would amuse him after the tensed moments. He says, 'let's see your point, Arrogance.'

'I believe there is always a way for us to bring down each of the enemies,' Arrogance explains. 'The Word of The Redeemer confirms that all people who think are giants should take heed lest they fall by our swords.'

'That's the point!' Disunity says, looking at Arrogance with irritation. 'All the giants are aware of this. So they know how to protect themselves against us. Don't pretend as if you don't know this!'

'Now listen, Disunity,' Dragon says, looking offended. 'You're not

19

to disunite us here. You're to disunite the giants. I agree with what Arrogance says. There is always a way to get down our enemies. It is up to everyone of you to find that way.' He gestures at Compromise. 'Take the report of Compromise for instance. As we are having this meeting, he is still working to get Brethren down. You all know the rules very well. One of them is: we don't give up on anyone, no matter who he is. As long as they are still in the kingdom of man, we must always find ways to destroy them!' He looks round at the council members. 'No go, mobilize your warriors and find ways to bring down the giants and reduce them to meat for me before they create more enemies for us or before we are done for!' He looks at each of them again. 'Have I made myself clear?'

'Yes, my lord,' each of them says.

Dragon leaves the place at once. Of course, he is going to and fro in the kingdom of man, looking for whom he will devour as meat.

CHAPTER FOUR

Sister Flirt lies restlessly on her bed at night, trying to catch some sleep. Recently, she is having problem sleeping because she is bordered about her life. She desperately needs a man in her life as her chances of getting a good husband are slipping away gradually.

She is in her late twenties, outstandingly beautiful, gentle and devoted Believer, so to say. She lived a reckless life at one time until a matured Believer called Faithful introduced her to The Redeemer who delivers her from the warriors of Dragon who are determined to destroy her.

The day Faithful introduced her to The Redeemer is a day to reckon with. Faithful who was then a potential giant Believer at that time was going round the kingdom to look for those under the bondage of Dragon. He met Sister Flirt who instantly fell in love with him and desired to sleep with him if he made the request.

Faithful smiled at her as he went to join her with the aim to share The Word with her.

She was sitting on a wooden bench under a free, having fresh air then. He stood in front of her with the smiles that seem to be part of his charms and said, 'hi, beloved one.'

She looked at him. He was good looking and tall. She appreciated his looks and concluded that she could date him if that was what he wanted.

'Can I have a seat?' He asked her in a friendly tone.

She thought he must be a perfect gentleman. She thought she was yet to meet someone like him. How could she anyway? She told herself. She was wild and irresponsible. So all the people - both males and females in her life were as wild as she was.

She returned the smile and gestured a space for him beside her. 'You can sit here.' Since she was dealing with a gentleman, she decided to play the gentle lady along side with him though she wondered how long it would take him to discover she was playing the chameleon.

'I am one of your lovers,' Faithful said gently.

Of course, Flirt raised an eyebrow, wondering how he becomes her lover. 'How do you mean, Sir?' She asked softly, still hiding her true colour.

'I mean I am one of those who love you,' he said. 'You are lovely because you're beautifully, wonderfully and fearfully created by God. God really invested a lot in you, you know. Out of millions of seed from your father, which fertilized your mother's egg in the womb before you're conceived, God has to pick the one that formed you. Isn't that wonderful?'

Flirt was a little stunned, wondering at such revelation. After a brief while, she smiled. 'That's the most wonderful things I have ever heard from anyone since I was born.'

'That's not the most wonderful thing I have for you,' Faithful said. 'I am actually sent to you by someone who loves you much more than anyone else.'

'Who else could that be except my mother?' she said.

'No. It's not your mother, my beloved sister,' he replied quickly. 'The person is a man. He did for you what nobody can do for you.'

'Who is that person?' Flirt asked anxiously.

'The person is a Crown Prince, the Heir to the throne of the Kingdom called Eternal Bliss, which has no beginning and no end.'

'A Crown Prince of Eternal Bliss?' she asked with a frown. 'I'm not sure I know anything about him or the Kingdom.'

'I'll tell you about him and the Kingdom,' Faithful said gently, 'if you spare me enough time to explain them to you and what they mean to you.' He hesitated for a while before he asked, 'Can you spare me the time to explain?'

'Yes, of course,' she replied quickly, curiously looking at him.

Faithful began gently and slowly, 'Before the Prince came into this kingdom, a Prophet called Isaiah said that a king shall reign in righteousness and that the Prince shall rule in judgment. When he eventually came into this kingdom, he started looking for you and me but we have all gone astray like sheep without a shepherd. We were in the camp of the enemies who plan to roast us in the lake that burns with fire and brimstone. The Prince went into the camp of the enemies even though he was not expected to be there. Because he loves us so much, he went there with the plan to redeem us from Dragon who keeps us there with heavy chain called sin. The Prince now goes about, looking for us, telling those that labour and are heavy laden to come to him. He is always ready to give us rest from all our pains and sorrows. He says that his sheep knows his voice. When they hear him, they would respond. I heard him and I responded. I went to him on my kneels and I talked with him. You know, he went through a lot before we are redeemed from Dragon who is very powerful. For the redemption to be complete, however, we have to receive the Prince into our lives and tell him we are sorry for all we have done wrong. After the Prince reconciles me with Eternal Father, he told me to go to other people like you and tell them that he is waiting to receive them like the case of prodigal son and his father. With what the Prince has done for us, I need to ask you if you think your mother can do any of these for you.'

Flirt looked thoughtful. She was actually moved by the story. She could not imagine the Prince to forsake all he has and come to this kingdom that is characterized with afflictions, depressions and oppressions of the enemies of the people. She replied, 'I don't think my mother can do a thing like for me or anyone.'

'Even then,' Faithful said, 'the Prince did much more. He was arrested for the offence he knows nothing about.'

'What?' She looked stunned. 'The people don't recognize him or what?'

'No,' Faithful said, 'they don't know him or what he means to them. Before some people knew him, they have already killed him like a common criminal.'

Sister Flirt stood up in rage. 'That's impossible!'

'Calm down, Sister Beloved.'

'My name is Flirt,' she corrected, sitting down thoughtfully. She was really furious at the people for killing someone that has come to relieve them of their heavy burden.

'I know your name is Flirt…'

'How do you know,' she asked curiously.

'I can see the name written in the cloths you're putting on. Only people with that name wear that kind of stuff.'

'I see.'

'But I know when your name is changed into Beloved, your dressing will change.'

'Who is going to change that?' she asked with amusement. 'Flirt I was when I was born.'

'When you become born-again, you shall be called by a new name. Then new things will begin to happen in your life.'

'You sound so sure,' she said with serious tone.

'I am sure because The Word never fails.'

'You can continue with your story about the Prince. It's really intriguing,' she said.

He paused after a while, thinking of where he left off. Then he continued, 'the Prince was killed like a criminal because he has to be killed.'

'Why does he deserve to die?' Flirt looked irritated.

'The prophesy of Isaiah has to be fulfilled. It was him that announced the Prince's death. In his prophecy about the Prince, he said, "But he was wounded for our transgressions, he was bruised for our iniquities: the chastisement of our peace was upon him; and with his stripes we are healed.

'All we like sheep have gone astray; we have turned every one to his own way; and the LORD hath laid on him the iniquity of us all.

'He was oppressed, and he was afflicted, yet he opened not his mouth: he is brought as a lamb to the slaughter, and as a sheep before her shearers is dumb, so he openeth not his mouth.

'He was taken from prison and from judgment: and who shall declare his generation? for he was cut off out of the land of the living: for the transgression of my people was he stricken.

'And he made his grave with the wicked, and with the rich in his death; because he had done no violence, neither was any deceit in his mouth.

'Yet it pleased the LORD to bruise him; he hath put him to grief: when thou shalt make his soul an offering for sin, he shall see his seed, he shall prolong his days, and the pleasure of the LORD shall prosper in his hand.

'He shall see of the travail of his soul, and shall be satisfied: by his knowledge shall my righteous servant justify many; for he shall bear their iniquities.

'In short, he has to die before he can actually redeem as many as believe in him.'

'I don't understand.' Flirt was really confused.

Faithful tried to explain. 'When he went into the grave, he actually went to fight our enemies that take our kingdom from our fore-parents and make us his slaves. The Prince's battle with our enemies in the grave took three long days. On the third day, the Prince took the key of freedom from the hands of our enemy, rose up from the grave and gives it to as many as believe in him. The key is called salvation and only the Prince can give it to us.'

'Are you talking about The Redeemer?' Flirt asked after a

thoughtful moment.

'Yes,' Faithful said in a whisper. 'The Redeemer has many names. He is the Prince of Peace, Wonderful, Counselor, Immanuel, Jesus Christ, the Lion of Judah, Saviour and others like that. We call him The Redeemer because He redeems as many as believe in Him. These include you and me.'

'You mean The Redeemer died because of me?' Flirt asked with sober reflection.

'Yes, Sister Beloved,' Faithful again whispered.

'Why didn't anyone tell me this before now?' She asked with guilt.

'You were told, sister Beloved,' he said. 'The mere fact that you mentioned his name proves that you've heard of him.'

'Yes,' she said quietly. 'I was told but I was not listening.'

'That's always the problem with most people who heard about him.' he said. Then he added cheerfully, 'but it's not too late for you to accept The Redeemer now. If you have crossed over to Eternity through death without having him as your Lord and Saviour, you'll be lost completely in the lake of fire. You can still make it to Eternal Bliss if you let The Redeemer come into your life just as he came into my life.'

'I want The Redeemer in my life.'

And so Flirt became a Believer that day. It took her time before she realized that being a Believer means going through a very rough journey. In fact, she had to go through storm; wilderness and even fierce battles as she struggles to maintain her salvation. She has fallen down as she climbed through the levels of maturity but The Redeemer is always there to lift her up. A matured Believer called Hope is a real vessel that was used by The Redeemer to strengthen her. Hope once told her that growing in The Spirit is similar to the growth in The Flesh. There are times in the life of a person when he learns to sit just as there are of periods of learning to stand and walk. Each of these times is always seemed to be characterized with sheer failures. If a child gives up learning to walk, the chances are that he would not be able to walk at the time others are walking. He may drag the period of walking to the time he is supposed to be running and climbing huddles. Similarly, if a babe Believer stops growing, he will never grow beyond the level of babes that feed only on milk. In fact, if he completely stops growing in The Spirit, he may start dying. So no one, according to Hope, must give up growing in The Spirit. No one, as a matter of fact, is too matured to grow in The Spirit. If a Believer grows from one level to another until he is more than a conqueror or a giant, Dragon will always reinforce the rulers of darkness against him. So no

25

Believer can afford to stop growing even at the level of a giant.

Flirt could not grow beyond the stage of babe Believer before she joins the meetings of Brethren. In spite of the balanced diet of The Word which Brethren often serves, she still battles with principalities that are fighting her in The Flesh and in The Mind. Instead of taking the battle to The Spirit where she can easily get victory, she is constantly lured through The Mind to The Flesh. Thus she is always faced with a warrior of Dragon called Lascivious Thoughts who always lies to her that Brethren is interested in her. He often times proves the lies to be true through Brethren's caring attitude. He points her attention to the gentle and loving way he speaks to her and the way he enjoys spending time with her.

Through the operation of Lascivious Thoughts, Flirt begins to look for evidence that proves that Brethren actually loves her, however false it may be. Of course, she gets the false evidence through the way he responds to her whenever she goes to him for counsel.

Lascivious Thoughts is able to lure her from The Mind to The Flesh where another member of Principalities called Masturbation is able to strike her with the first blow. Of course, she falls down. Because she hangs on the passage of The Word that assures her that if she falls, she will stand again, she is able to stand. The first blow from any of the enemies, however, is usually the hardest and most dangerous one. To survive it, the Believer would need a giant Believer by his or her side. Instead of calling for help after standing on her feet again, she relies on her strength, which is no strength at all. She is weak but she manages to stand. Masturbation strikes again and again. Each time, she tries to stand up. She calls on The Redeemer to help her. The way she wants him to help her is not in line with The Word. She wants him to tell Brethren to marry her even though she knows he is married. She feels she needs Brethren who is a giant as a husband. With him as her husband, she knows she can easily grow into a giant too.

The Redeemer does not seem to hear her because what she is asking for is contrary to The Word, which says: one man, one wife - for better, for worse - two and not three people become one flesh. Asking The Redeemer to make her Brethren's wife is obviously influenced by one of The Rulers of Darkness called Ignorance. Actually, the involvement of The Rulers of Darkness in her case is with the purpose of using her as a bait to bring down Brethren, the real target.

Having been reduced by Masturbation into a sickly Believer who is dying gradually in The Spirit, Fornication goes to her in the form of Good Idea. He tells her of a way out of the problem, suggesting to her to invite Brethren into her room, saying, 'if you tell him you are not feeling fine, he will come to you in the house with the intention to bring you back to shape. When he comes, you can let him see how beautiful your body is. Then he can decide whether to have you or not. If he tries to argue about having two wives, you can tell him about other giants like David whom they read about in The Word. Solomon is also another good example that has many wives. You can ask him, what is the big deal if all he has are just two wives?'

Sister Flirt nods with understanding and decides to follow the plan of Good Idea.

CHAPTER FIVE

Brethren is with his wife, trying to play love with her. His wife who is called Mrs. Levity Brethren is a very lovely and loving woman. She loves her husband very much even though she often times finds his demand of her womanhood obscene. She feels everything about a Believer should be done with moderation. Only things of The spirit should be taken to the extreme although when she needs a baby, she knows how to constantly place demand of his manhood. Whenever he wants to enjoy himself with her, she either excuse herself by saying she is The spirit or she simply tells him she is not in the mood. Although Brethren can endure, being a giant but the unromantic attitude of his wife is really growing into a big torn in his body. Having a torn in his body makes him a little vulnerable to the attack in The Flesh even though Levity does not seem to understand this. He tires to explain to her in a gentle manner what he is going through. Sometimes she understands. Other times she cannot imagine a giant like him becoming vulnerable. 'You are meant to relieve me of the pain that is brought about by the torn in my flesh,' he tells her one day.

'If giants like Apostle Paul in The Word who had no wife can survive the torn, you too can,' she replies.

'You're the grace I have,' Brethren says. More often than not, Brethren has to use The Word to teach her her roles on their matrimonial bed before she relieves him.

Brethren is now trying to make his wife be in the mood but this time she tells him point blank that she is too tired to dance to his music of love.

While thinking of what else to do, a message is sent to him by one of Believers that comes regularly to the meetings. According to the message, the sister is not feeling fine. She is afflicted by something she cannot understand. So she needs his help in her house.

Brethren at once goes to the house of the Believer whom he

28

knows as a very devoted follower of The Redeemer. She often goes to him for counseling. Her love for the Redeemer is really worth the effort of going to help her out of the affliction.

Sister Flirt is the only person in the room when Brethren enters the house through the door that leads to the sitting room.

'Hello,' Brethren calls when he finds the sitting room empty. 'Is anyone at home?'

'I'm … inside here …' He hears Flirt's quiet voice coming from one of the rooms. He goes to the room and knocks.

'Please… come, in, sir,' the same quiet voice responds.

Quietly he opens the door. Sister Flirt is on the bed, completely naked though she is covered with a blanket. 'How are you, sister?' He asks in a gentle voice.

'I'm not feeling fine, sir,' she replies. 'I'm under serious attack.'

'So I was told,' Brethren says, moving closer to sit on the only chair in the small room. It is close to the bed.

'Why are you all by yourself, sister?'

'I have no one to look after me,' she replies, looking as if she is going to cry.

'I'm so sorry,' Brethren said quietly. 'I know Comforter will comfort you in the name of Jesus.'

'Amen. Thank you, sir.'

'So what's the problem?' He asks

'It's a battle, sir.'

'In which of the battlefields, my sister?

'It's the one in The Flesh,' she replies. 'I need a giant as my husband and Comforter tells me to tell you.'

He looks thoughtful for a while before he said, 'Perhaps He wants me to pray with you. Or what does He expects me to do? I mean we are supposed to tell Him what we want.'

'I think he wants you to lay your hand on the wounded part of my body.'

Brethren frowns. In all the years of his walk with Comforter, he has never been given such instruction. 'Are you sure of this, sister?'

'Yes, sir.'

'Which part of your body if I may ask?'

'I will show you,' she says. Before he can say another word, she is on her feet. She goes to lock the door and walks to him in the nude, looking at him with seductive expressions.

Now Brethren knows he had walked into a trap. Getting out is a problem - a very big one. Every part of his body yearns to have a taste

29

of her. He closes his eyes, hoping to resist the temptation through that but the memory of the naked beautiful lady is still there. While closing his eyes, a passage in The Word keeps ringing in his head, "flee from fornication!"

Without opening his eyes, he says, 'sister, please, don't do this to me. I have a covenant with The Redeemer that the day I'm knocked down by Adultery, I would ask him to take me home.'

'But Comforter says you should lay your hand on the wounded part of my body.'

'Where is that?' Brethren asks without opening his eyes. He hopes it would be the part he can touch. If it is, he will put his hand there and then requests her to let him leave.

'It's... em... my reproductive organ.'

'Comforter can't say a thing like that!'

'Why not?'

'It contradicts The Word.'

'Then who has been talking to me?'

'It's the messengers of the Dragon,' he says impatiently. 'You are supposed to know that if you're familiar with The Word.'

'I see...' Flirt says reluctantly. As she is about to change her mind about sleeping with him by all means, the Rulers of Darkness assemble in the room without any visible appears. Of course, Brethren can perceive them. He starts quoting The Word to them without making himself audible. 'When the enemies come against me, Comforter shall lift up a standard against them. Because I am following The Word, saying that if a man looks lustfully at a woman, he has committed adultery with her in his heart, The Redeemer will make me overcome.'

'Brethren,' Compromise says but Flirt cannot hear nor see him. She can only hear warriors in the class of Principalities. 'You're such a fool. Your wife never gives you what is rightfully yours - her body. She leaves you alone in the rain with pain without gain of marriage. Would you call your union with her marriage or mirage? Think, Brethren, if you have this beautiful lady only this once, it's okay.'

'Once is more than enough to destroy someone like me,' Brethren replies aloud, still closing his eyes.

'What?' Flirt asks.

'I'm not talking to you.'

'Then who are you talking to?'

'I think it's a ruler of darkness.'

'There's no ruler of darkness here,' she tells him. 'I always talk to

Comforter here.'

'You're not talking to Comforter,' he replies her. 'You're talking to the warrior of Dragon. The only way you can know is through The Word of The Redeemer. The voice of Comforter cannot contradict The Word in any way.'

'Let's go into The Word if that's the way you want it,' Ignorance says.

Brethren cannot really distinguish who is who through their voices. He can only know who through what he says. He knows the first speaker is Compromise who is good at giving excuses while indulging in sins. He is also good at destroying people's abilities to control their desires, impulses and emotions. He always seeks for ways to transfer aggression from the real enemies to the vessels they use to provoke and destroy relationships, including marriages.

'Let me remind you of men in The Word that married hundreds of wives. A typical example is Solomon who had up to one thousand women in his life.'

'The Redeemer says it's not so from the beginning. In the first marriage in this kingdom, there s only one man one wife.'

Flirt hears him again but she decides not to interrupt him. Perhaps through what he is saying, she can know what he and Comforter decides about her case.

Disobedience says, 'Brethren, so many things are going on among Believers like you. Many of them are far stronger than you. The men are keeping mistresses even with the knowledge of their wives. I'm surprised you don't consider having another woman in your life. It's a light thing to do.'

'I have a covenant. So I can't do it.'

'Yes, I know you have a covenant. The Redeemer is the only one that never breaks covenant but the situation you find yourself can make you break it. You know he'll understand. He's a loving and merciful Being who is always ready to forgive and forget.

There is a quiet voice which sounds like that of Comforter, 'don't dialogue with your enemies. The Word says, "Flee from Fornication." Deliverance from Fornication is not in dialogue. It is in your legs. Leave now!'

Brethren stands up slowly, still closing his eyes. 'Sister, where are you?

'I'm there, sir.'

'I saw you locking the door. Can you open it, please?'

'You mean you're not going to touch me, sir?' She asks in an appealing voice.

'No, I can't,' he says. 'I'm sorry. It's not Comforter that talked to you. It's the enemy of Believers. They just spoke to me too. I really can't blame you if you fall for their lies. They are very persuasive and can convince you that they are Comforter.

'I can't let you go without doing anything to be. At least, you have to prove to me that you're not going to hate me for trying to tempt you.'

'You know I'll never hate someone I love, most especially the person The Redeemer died for.' There is a thoughtful silence. Brethren misunderstands her silence as a sign of disbelief. He added after a while, 'I promise to kiss your cheek if put on your cloths and open the door.

Flirt smiles. 'Okay,' she says and goes to put on her cloths. She opens the door, standing by the entrance. 'You can open your eyes now.'

'Can I still trust you?'

'Yes, sir.'

He opens his eyes a last and smiles. 'Thank you.'

'I'm sorry I tried to pull you down,' she whispers.

'It's okay,' he says to her. 'It's not your making. The enemies just want to use you against me because they know I love you.'

She looks a little surprised. 'You love me?'

'Yes, of course,' he whispers. 'I love you with the love of The Redeemer. That's why I'm here. If you need me again, I'll still come here.'

'You really mean it?'

He nods, smiling.

'After all I tried to do you?'

'Please, don't blame yourself. It's not you. The battle actually started before coming here. I am the target, not you. Since I have not fallen, you have not fallen.'

She marvels at him. 'What… kind of man are you?'

'I'm a servant of The Redeemer who is to ensure that none of His sheep go astray. I must not take advantage of anyone that is weak. What happened now does not mean you're not a Believer. You just need to grow above this level so that you will not be manipulated by the enemies and used against a Believer like you. I'm sure you understand why I have to keep loving you in spite of it all.'

She bursts into emotional sobs, saying, 'I wish with my heart that The Redeemer gives me a man like you as a husband… I will never ask for anything more.'

'He will give you your heart desire but you must understand that if you are going to marry someone like me, you have to build yourself up through faith and self discipline.'

'Is that all I need to do to get a man like you?'

'Comforter will teach you the rest.'

She smiles. 'Thank you, sir.' She looks at him as he makes attempt to go. 'How about your promise, sir?'

He kisses her on the cheek and smiles. 'We'll see at the meeting.'

'Okay, sir.'

He leaves the house, feeling victorious. He knows he just defeats the rulers of darkness through Comforter who helps him overcome temptation.

CHAPTER SIX

Dragon looks angrily at the rulers of darkness who all fell like bunch of failures. 'You let Brethren get out of the hook after going that far with him?' There is a long uncomfortable silence. 'You all amaze me.'

'Actually, my lord,' Compromise attempts to explain, 'Comforter foils our plans to get him down.

'That's not an excuse!' Dragon roars with fury. 'I told you times without number to ensure that our victim first grieves Comforter before you strike him. How do you expect to get a giant like Brethren down without first driving away Comforter. You think he's a cheap rat like Flirt who is almost dead in The spirit?' Again, there is a long silence as he calms down a little. He knows anger cannot solve the problem, however fierce. Besides his council members need to be encouraged. After all, they almost get Brethren down if not for the mistake they make. 'Well,' he says with a deep sigh, 'you would have brought him down if not for the mistake. I don't want you to give up on him.'

'We really need your help if we have to go after him again,' Compromise says. 'We all know that the victory over us will strengthen him the more.

Dragon grins, showing his ugly teeth. It is apparent that the grin is not a sigh of amusement but it is hard to tell if he is irritated or not. 'You don't need my help in this matter. There are millions of cases I have to attend to. I have to be making cases against other giants as you know I can only be in one place at a time. I have you to operate in so many ways so that humans may feel I'm omnipresent like The Father in Eternity.' The moment the thought of Eternity occurs to him, his countenance changes. There is dead silence. The rulers of darkness immediately sense what is going on in his mind.

Dragon reflects how the whole scenarios began. It started when he tried to carry out the plan to create a kingdom within the kingdom of the Father. That time he was one of the top messengers of The Father, the King of in Eternity kingdom, which has no beginning and no end. He leads other to adore The Father. There were great unity, bliss, love, joy and so many wonderful things back then until he decided that he wanted to have his own kingdom. He began to rebel against The Father, converting so many other messengers to his side. Then he launched a way against The Father. Since The Father cannot tolerate such rebellion in his kingdom, he assigned another arch messenger called Michael to deal with him. The war in Eternity was great until Dragon and all his messenger were thrown out of the kingdom into the kingdom that was then without form or shape. It was void and dark upon the face of the deep. This dark kingdom was not actually intended for Dragon and his messengers. The Father re-made the dark kingdom into a far better one through The Word that was then inside him. Each day of the six days, The Father sent The Word who came out through his mouth to do the work of recreation. After the six days, The Word had to rest because he has done so much work. When the dark kingdom had been transformed, The Father gave it to the first couple called Adam and Eve. They and their children were supposed to have dominion all over the place.

No one can really tell at which period, the kingdom of Doom which is made up of lake that burns with fire and brimstone was made by The Father but it is assumed that it is shortly after Dragon was kicked out of heaven. Invariably, there are three kinds of kingdom which are the kingdom of The father in Eternity, the kingdom of man and the kingdom of Doom. The kingdom of Doom was initially made for Dragon and his messengers who were determined to have their own kingdom. Of course, the kingdom of Doom is full of horrors, leaving Dragon frustrated and envious of man who was made the king of the earth. Out of vengeance against The Father and fury, Dragon decided to annex the kingdom of man to his kingdom in Doom and reduce all humans into slaves that would toil from day till night through out their lives. After each of them departs from the earth, he or she end up in Doom Kingdom.

Dragon went to Eve in the form of friendly serpent to have a chat with her. He was able to take over the kingdom of man through her and her husband by making them to violate the law of dominion that were given to them. As soon as Dragon takes over the kingdom, he makes all humans slaves in the kingdom where they are supposed to rule as kings and queens. With Dragon in change, things are never the same for everybody that is born of a man and a woman. The spirit of death

35

begins to kill everyone on earth after other soldiers of Dragon like Lust Of The Flesh, Lust Of The Eyes and Pride Of Life who has different ways of destroying people with spiritual and Eternal deaths. Spiritual death is actually the death in the battlefield of The Epirit while Eternal Death is in the one in Doom.

Doom, the kingdom created by The Father for Dragon and his warrior messengers but they decided that they need as many subjects as possible. So the only place they can get subjects is in the kingdom of man. Dragon and his warriors not only enslave the people but also take them to Doom where he will rule over them forever.

The Father is not happy because he does not desire the eternal death of the people but for them to have eternal life. Eternal life is actually the life in Eternal kingdom of The Father. Even though The Father never wanted to interfere with the kind of life man chooses, he knows that it is very necessary to let everybody know what is going on in the three kingdoms - kingdom of Eternity, the kingdom of man and Doom kingdom. Since man can perceive things only within his environment, he needs to be educated about the two others kingdoms which cannot be easily perceived with any of the human senses. If he is educated, he would be in a good position to decide where he will spend his eternity.

When The Father gave Adam and Eve the power to choose, they did not realize the danger in the power until Dragon helped them to use it in the way that brought woes to the entire mankind. Thus everybody on earth becomes enslaved by Dragon through the use of chains of bondage called sins and iniquities. Because The Father loves mankind so much, he feels the need to send someone who would come like a lamb that would break the chain of bondage and then set the people free. Before the lamb can do that, however, he would need to go through so much pains and sorrow, including going to face Dragon in Doom kingdom, taking him the key of freedom which he would need to break the chain of bondage. This will take three days of battle with Dragon in the grave.

The nature of this mission demands much more than anyone in either the kingdom of The Father or kingdom of the man can offer. Dragon knows that no one can possibly redeem the people from him, no matter how powerful he is. The reason is that he has legal ground to rule the people and The Father, being just, recognizes that. This is what gives Dragon the confidence that no one could come to him in Doom and take the key unless, of course, The Father leaves his throne in Eternity and come to him. Since he did not see the reason

The Father would do a crazy thing like that, Dragon concluded that the people do not have any chance of being redeemed from him.

Love who is one of the living attributes of The Father constantly worried The Father to do something to save mankind from Dragon until he decided that he would go by himself through The Word who formed the kingdom of man. Before the execution of the wonderful decision, it was made known to man through a prophet called Isaiah that a child that would save mankind would be born. Again, before this time, The Word who lives inside The Father had never been separated from him except during the time of creation the kingdom of man and all the things inside.

When it was time to carry out the plan of redemption, The Word entered the womb of a virgin called Mary and she became pregnant. In spite of all Dragon did to stop the birth of the promised child, The Word came into the kingdom of man and become The Redeemer of mankind

Shortly before The Redeemer began his mission in the kingdom of man, Dragon had the chance to abort it through temptations. He took him to a high place and showed the Redeemer all the kingdom of man and said, 'all these I will give you if only you would bow down before me.'

Although The Redeemer must have been amused at the thought of bowing down to Dragon - a created being, he did not disprove the fact that the kingdom of man had been handed over to him by man himself. Dragon, however, failed to realize that The Redeemer is from The Father who knows that he took the kingdom from man by crook and trick. Of course, all his plans to get The Redeemer on his side failed.

He soon discovered that he had aided The Redeemer to accomplish his mission on earth by making the people to kill him like a common criminal. Passing through the grave for three long days, The Redeemer went to Dragon in Doom kingdom and took the key of Salvation from him. On the third day, he came back to the kingdom of man and becomes The Great Redeemer, the Lord of lords and the Saviour of mankind, handing the key to as many as believe in him. Invariably, the people with the key of Salvation are those who are actually free from the bondage of Dragon.

The Redeemer later left the kingdom of man for Eternity kingdom to prepare mansions for those who believes in him. He later sent them Comforter who is also from Eternity to give as many as believe in him power, making them children of God. He also gives them the whole amour of war, making every Believer, no matter how small a threat to Doom kingdom and also to his operations in the kingdom of man.

Dragon signs with sudden change of expressions after he briefly recalls what has happened in the past. He cannot understand the reason The Father loves the people so much to the extent of sending His only Begotten Son to redeem them from him. The people are ordinary dust. What makes them different from animals, as far as he knows, is the breath of The Father that forms their spirits. Even then the breath would be taken away from them sooner or later and their flesh will return to dust, leaving their souls to face the judgment of The Father on the day of reckoning. Furthermore, he is yet to understand why The Father goes as far as giving them Comforter who will strengthen and help them win the battle, which they can never win on their own, giving them the whole armour of war that will earn them victories. With Comforter and the amour of war, the smallest among Believers is big enough to level his combined forces. If not for his council members that make the people ignorant of their strengths and the war against them in The Spirit, The Flesh and The mind; the battle ought to have come to an end before it begins at all.

Dragon looks at his council members and says, 'I can't get involved in the battle directly. You know that, don't you? I have to constantly go to The Father to accuse as many Believers that violate the rules he has given them while you continue to influence them to break law the more. This is one of the best way to bring our enemies down. You know it is essentially through the violation of the rules that we can disarm and make them vulnerable and easy even for the smallest of our warriors to strike them dead. I know by the time we are through with terrorist Brethren, we would have reduced him into meat for a warrior like Adultery to devour.'

'I don't think anyone here knows how a small warrior like Adultery can bring down a terrorist like Brethren,' Ignorance says. 'I feel we are dealing with an immutable giant that simply refuses to die either in The Spirit or in The Mind.'

'So what are you suggesting?' Dragon is irritated. 'You want us to give up on him and allow him to turn our slaves against us, eh?'

Everyone is dead silent.

Dragon senses their fear. So he calms down and says, 'the long and short of it is that we can kill him in The Flesh,'

The warrior cannot hide their surprise. They wonder if Dragon expects The Redeemer to take him to Eternity just like that at the time he is been used to set the slaves free from them.

Dragon says. 'I've checked on him. He's having a covenant with The Father. He told The Redeemer that he would like to be taken to Eternity before he falls as a giant In any of the battlefields. The implication of that is: if we cannot stop his activities in the kingdom of man, we can compel The Redeemer to take him away before he ruins everything we've building over the millennia.'

'That's going to be very hard to do,' Compromise says 'Don't forget, my lord, The Redeemer has few warriors that are making exploits for him in this kingdom. Reducing their number by calling any of them home, especially giants like Brethren is going to be very hard for him to do. I mean - think of what it has taken The Redeemer before he could train him into a giant.'

'Listen to me,' Dragon says, 'If you know where to strike, nobody is too great for us to bring down.'

'Tell us where to strike, master,' the members say almost at the same time.

'Strike him though his wife by making her to deny him of the benefits of marriage. After striking him long enough, Flirt can be brought in again. Through that, you can get him down.'

The council members cheer Dragon for the brilliant idea. After a while, the meeting ends.

CHAPTER SEVEN

Brethren looks at his wife, Levity who lies beside him; looking at the other side trying to catch some sleep. She just refuses to allow him to touch her again, complaining of headache which he is almost sure is an excuse to deny him again of what is rightfully his.

He feels like telling her of the temptation Comforter helps him to overcome but he decides against it, knowing fully well that Sister Flirt will be implicated. As a leader in the Fellowship, he always feels the need to protect the images of others even though each of them makes mistakes at one time or the other. He is aware that the rulers of darkness simply want to use the sister to bring him down from the level he is operating in The Spirit. Sister Flirt is either a babe or sickly Believer who needs help. So he cannot use what she tries to do as way to get what he needs from his wife. So instead of bringing her in, he decides to educate his wife of the dreadful implications of the denial of his rights on their matrimonial bed.

'Honey,' he says softly.

Levity does not respond. She knows he is about to appeal to her and she is not in the mood to hear any of his sermons that will change her mind.

'I know you're not asleep yet,' he continues.

'I'm trying to catch some sleep here,' she snaps.

'I'm sorry but can we talk bout this - please?'

'What do you want us to talk about at the time we are supposed to be sleeping?'

'Can I have your attention just for a moment - please?'

She sits up and leans on her back on the bed. He does the same, trying to hold her hand. She withdraws her hand almost immediately. 'I thought you have something important to say.'

'Yes,' he says. "First of all, I want to say I love you very much. God gave you to me as my wife and I have no other woman but you....'

40

'Please, cut the long sermon short, I need some sleep,' she interrupts him.

'Okay,' he says after a sign. 'I... em... feel I should first tell you how much I appreciate before I tell you that there is a serious battle against me.'

That catches her attention as she looks at him briefly.

'The battle is between me and the rulers of darkness who want to pull me down by all means.'

'Every Believer faces battle in that regards. So what's the big deal about your kind of battle?'

'How would you feel,' he asks, 'if you find someone like me on top of another woman.'

'Well, I'll simply classify you as one of the fake Believers.'

'Don't you think that'll be too judgmental on your part.'

'I'm not judgmental,' she replies immediately. 'The Word says that by their fruits you'll know them. If a Believer exhibits the fruit of adultery, that means he's not real.'

'You believe a Believer cannot fall, don't you?'

She is silent for a while before she replies, 'only babes will fall ad stand again but you're not a babe, are you?'

'The word of The Redeemer say that whoever thinks he stands should take heed least he falls. How do you interpret that passage in line with what we are talking about?'

There is a brief silence as she says slowly, 'you're the giant. You tell me.'

'You're also a giant. You just don't know it. Ignorance of whom we are sometimes makes us act below expectations.'

'Okay,' she admits, 'any Believer can fall if he is not careful. So what is the point?'

'The point is I'm a making, honey,' he says. 'I still live in the body. If you pitch me in the body, I'll feel the pain. If I see the naked body of a woman, I can be really tempted, especially if I've starved of what I need.'

'You talk as if this thing is food you're supposed to eat everyday.'

'Even if I can't eat it everyday, let me have it when I need it.'

'That's the problem with you!' she says with irritation. 'You're selfish - you lack consideration for others.'

Brethren is almost provoked. He feels like telling her she is the one who is selfish and mean but he can perceive one of the warriors of Dragon called Wrath, operating. He calms down and he says as gentle as possible. 'I'm not selfish, honey. I'm only telling you I can fall

41

because I am still a man. If I fall, I'm a dead man.' He closes his eyes, trying to control the feeling of frustration inside him. 'I have a covenant with The Redeemer that the day I fall, I'll ask him to forgive me and take me to Eternity.'

'If you fall just like anyone can,' she says, 'The Word says you'll stand again.'

Brethren cannot believe she says a thing like that. He looks at her sharply. 'What do you mean?'

'I mean you can't scare me with that.'

'I don't believe you can say that,' he says. 'Do you think anyone who falls ever remains the same again even after standing?'

'Yes, I believe so because The Word says that with The Father all things are possible.'

'I think you're interpreting that passage to suit your purpose,' he says. 'Perhaps I should put it this way: do you think if someone like me fall, I will fall alone?'

She is silent, looking thoughtful.

'The answer is obviously no!' he tells her, smiling indulgently. 'Do you think my life is all about me?'

Again there is silence.

'You have to understand that someone like me cannot afford to just stand, let alone to fall. I have to constantly be on the move as a warrior of The Redeemer. Obviously, if Dragon gets someone like me down, which is his target anyway, many would go down with me. Even if I stand as you are trying to tell me, do you think people that fall as a result of my falling will stand again? Think about this, honey: my falling is not my falling alone but that of many others and my struggle is not my struggle alone but that of many others because I'm not living for myself. I am living for The Redeemer and I am living for the people I am leading to Eternity kingdom. This is war - war in The Flesh, war in The Spirit and war in The Mind. We are all fighting all these wars and we are supposed to help one another to win these wars, not to give room for the enemies to defeat any of us. You better make the sacrifice that is required of you so that you can make up for my weakness. If you think that still doesn't matter to you, it's okay. But you must understand that if you let me fall into the hands of another woman, you're already a widow.'

He lies down again, covers himself with the blanket as if he is about to go to sleep.

Levity thinks about what he says for a while. Then she asks herself, 'what on earth is wrong with me? I must be under attack too.

Whatever makes me treat my loving husband like this is definitely not from Comforter. If it's not from Comforter, it must be from the rulers of darkness.' Tears blind her eyes as she lays her hand on her husband's shoulder. He does not respond. 'I'm sorry, my love.'

'I've talked to The Redeemer about you. He has forgiven you. That's all that counts,' he says. 'You can go back to sleep.'

'You have to forgive me too.'

He looks at her with slight surprise. 'You know I'll never hold any grudge against you, don't you?'

'I know but you have to love me now.'

'I love you, of course,' he says. 'I told you that before the conversation, didn't I?'

'You can prove it to me now,' she says, 'and anytime you want to.'

He looks at her with smiles. Without waiting for him to say or do anything again, she hugs him, kissing him while he caresses her body. Both of them begin to explode with passionate love for each other.

Since that day, Levity sees herself as a shield against the arrows of Lust Of Flesh through which the enemies plan to get her husband down. Whenever he makes a demand of total submission of her body anytime and anywhere, she always brings herself into the mood. Whenever she feels like refusing him, she will instantly perceive the rulers of darkness at work. Before long, she begins to grow, fighting along side with her husband in The Spirit and in The Mind where they usually get victories after victories.

The rulers of darkness retrieve from the couple for a while and had an emergency meeting. Dragon is not available to preside over the meeting. He is busy going to and fro in kingdom of man and Eternity kingdom, accusing Believers of iniquities before The Father.

'Sometimes I wonder if master knows anything about the terrorist we are dealing with here,' Disobedience asks the rest of the rulers of darkness when they are discussing the issue of Brethren.

'Better hang it there,' Ignorance says. 'And we'll pretend as if we didn't hear you.'

'Why?' Disobedience asks in frustration. 'Do you want us to pretend as if we don't know what just happened?'

'What happened?' Compromise asks as if he does not know.

'You want me to spell it out to you that we just failed?'

Compromise looks puzzled. 'Did we?'

'See, what I mean?' Disobedience asks the rest.

'We don't see things the way you see them, Disobedience,' Disunity says. 'What you see as failure is actually a chance to try again and again until we succeed.'

'Really?' Disobedience says. 'That's a strong proof that you're more ignorant than Ignorance.'

'Well,' Disunity says. 'I'll accept it if you can prove it with just one strong point.'

'Okay,' Disobedience says. 'We did not only fail to bring Brethren down but also succeeded in making Levity stronger and more careful than before. With the way she is fighting our warriors alongside with her husband right now, we are building her into a giant!'

'I see,' Disunity says. 'If that's your point, you really don't have any.'

'Really?' Disobedience asks. 'Let's see your point if you have any.'

Although all the council members know that there will be no room for the argument if Dragon is around but they all consider the debate as a way of seeing where things go wrong. So they allow each of them to present their points and counter points.

'I'm not going to counter your point,' Disunity says, 'I'll simply refresh your poor memory with the point I am about to present. We have been involved in the battle of the conquerors where I made conquerors to fight one another, using the weapon they are supposed to use against us. The more giants we have, the easier it is for me to operate. Once I'm involved in the battle, I can make it easy for our warriors in the least category of principalities to strike them down. All I need before I maneuver the battle in our favour is Wrath, Doctrinal Differences, Variance, Individualism and even Denominationalism. Before they know it, the so-called giants or conquerors will be fighting one other instead of fighting us.'

Not willing to accept defeat, Disobedience says, 'then why is it so difficult for you or your combined forces to tackle Brethren if you're so smart?'

'Patience is the hallmark of victory in this battle,' Disunity tells him. 'Check the history of all Believers and find out which of them get all victories. At one time or the other, each of them had been defeated.'

'Really?' Disobedience argues. 'Why is it that all giants are so strong?'

'They are strong only when they come together. If they don't, any of them can be defeated. As you know, the defeat of one is the defeat of the rest of them.'

Compromise says, 'warriors, we're not getting anywhere with this argument.' He looks at Disobedience. 'You know the master will not tolerate the way you're talking but we'll pretend as if you did not say this. Apparently, we can't give up on Brethren. The master always tells us that giving up on anyone is not an option. So we must keep fighting Brethren and his wife until we get him down. Do we agree to this?'

'Yes,' most of them reply.

'What do you think?' Compromise asks Disobedience.

'I think we have to know the status of whom we're dealing with,' he replies. 'If we don't know this, it's going to be hard if not impossible to bring him down.'

'You're right,' Compromise says. 'At least, we can see that you agree that we can always get down our victims.' He looks round at the rest before he asks, 'what's the status of our victim?'

'Well,' Disunity says. 'From the information I have while working on how to strike the couple, Levity is not a babe Believer. She is a warrior but not yet a giant.'

'Are you so sure of that?' Arrogance who is silent all the while asks.

'I have one of my warriors called Backbiting checking on the couple,' Disunity replies.

'How are you going to strike them now?' Arrogance asks.

Disunity smiles. He knows he must have offended him when he tells the rest about his achievements. In order to give him a sense of relevance, he says, 'you're going to strike Brethren and his wife this time. We'll take orders from you as far as this case is concerned.'

All the rulers of darkness look at Arrogance, wondering how he is going to react.

Of course, Arrogance is inwardly happy. The mere fact that he gets their attention is enough to take up the challenge even though he knows how dangerous the mission is.

'Let me see what I can do,' he says.

The rest gives him a big round of applause, making him to swell with excitements.

CHAPTER EIGHT

Arrogance begins to execute his plans to strike Brethren dead in The Spirit. He raises up some Believers in the class of babes to stand up against him at Fellowship. Most of these Believers are youths who do not know much about battles in The Flesh, The Spirit and The Mind. To them, having The Redeemer is all that counts. Hence, being bugged down by The Word is never part of their lifestyles. They feel that Eternity is sure for them because they have head-knowledge to direct them instead of The Word. They know they are the future leader. They, therefore, want to lead the older generations even though they do not have what it takes to lead.

Arrogance sends his warriors like Ego, Academics, Unteachable Spirit, Wisdom Of Man, Philosophies, Psychology and a lost of others to invade the youths in The mind, making them to live in The Flesh. The activities of the youths make the leading of the people to Eternity difficult for Brethren. This brings about argument about the pattern of the congregation. Disunity is immediately invited by Arrogance to disorganized them and put them in disarray. When Brethren tries to bring peace into the situation through the use of The Word, the babe believers criticize him and call him names like Holy-Old-Bag, Uncultured, Uncivilized, Old-Fashioned and even Idiot.

Arrogance speaks to Brethren in the secret, asking him, 'can you imagine those riff-raffs calling you names? When were they born, when did they know The Redeemer and what gives them the rights to call you names. They say you're stupid. You really must be stupid to have taken such insults from those good for nothing people who call themselves Believers.'

Brethren is really provoked but he knows what to do. He takes The Word and reads the passage in First Corinthians Chapter 4 verse10 that says, 'We are fools for Christ's sake, but ye are wise in Christ; we are weak, but ye are strong; ye are honourable, but we are despised.'

He smiles at himself after reading the place. He knows the poeple are right to call him an idiot. He is truly an idiot for the sake of The Redeemer. He decides to let everybody knows that.

During the next meeting, he wears a T-shirt with a bold tag: I am a FOOL" with smaller letters that read: for the sake of The Redeemer. He wears a coat over the T-shirt so that the people may not see the tag at the back.

When people, especially the babes Believers see the tag: 'I am a FOOL," they laugh at him. When he is about to share The Word with the people, he removes the coat and turns his back at them so that they can read question at the back of the T-shirt which asks; "whose FOOL are you?" Then he begins to share The Word. 'I have been called by so many names even by people that are Believers like me. I told The Redeemer that I am hurt by those names but he tells me that he was called a much more terrible names. He was called a criminal, prince of demons, blasphemer and all sorts of names you can image. He tells me in The Word that I should not expect the people to call me better names. Comforter directs me to read First Corinthians 4:10 'where I discovered that all those who have called me Idiot are not wrong after all because The Word says I am truly a fool for the sake of the Redeemer. Then I further concluded that everybody is a fool something or someone. So many things, especially things we cannot see are making fools out of us. Some are fools for opposite sex, some for materialism and some for arrogance and other warriors of Dragon. The truth is we are all fools. The difference between those fools are the different things that make each of us fools. That is the reason I ask the question in my T-shirt, "whose fool are you?

He moves closer to the people who are all dead silence. They can all perceive the aura of Comforter around him through the presence of Humility and Wisdom. This makes them respect him the more. 'If Dragon only makes us tools and leave us at that stage, that would have been tolerable. Comforter would simply take out our foolishness with the sue of The Word. But Dragon does not only makes fools out of us but also makes us his slaves and victims of his frustrations! He has dug a big grave in Doom and plans to bury as many as give the chance to carry out his plans. Guess what? He is having upper hand in this matter. If not, why it is that Believers like me, my own brothers and sisters that The redeemer gives to me as my family that are attacking me?' He bursts into tears. In the midst of his tears, he continues, 'I labour so that it is well with every one, knowing

47

fully well that your pains are my pains, your battles are my battles, your joy is my joy and your victories are my victories as well. Why, my brothers and sisters! Why stabbing me at the back with the same weapons we are supposed to use against our enemies? We are supposed to use our months to encourage one another, not to destroy each other. We are supposed to use the gifts The Redeemer has given us to expand the kingdom of The Father, and not to use it to reduce it...'

By the time Brethren finishes sharing The Word, there is no one that is not broken down. Before the end of the meeting, most of the babe Believers had become so matured that they are all ready to die just to fight along side with Brethren who they now see as their father in The spirit although not in The Flesh or the mind.

Dragon feels the great impact of Brethren's activities in The Spirit that day. The people at the meetings launch a heavy attack against his warriors as they come together chasing them in hundreds of thousands. The babe Believers who are once battling with principalities and now chasing the warriors that are in the levels of powers and even rulers of darkness.

He immediately leaves the courtroom that is located in The Spirit where he is making allegations against some strong Believers. The Father is The Judge while the Redeemer is The Advocate for the accused Believers. Dragon, of course is the accuser.

He calls for emergency meetings with ruler of darkness and demands what is happening. 'I heard a bomb shell in my kingdom and I see babe Believers chasing warriors in the class of powers and rulers of darkness. What exactly is going wrong here?'

Disobedience is the one that explains what actually happens. He tries to excuse himself by saying, 'I told them Brethren is not that easy to overcome.'

'What's the assignment I gave you about this man?' He demands angrily.

'You told us to strike him through his wife,' Disunity replies. 'We tried it but we fail.'

'Now you're admitting you failed?' Disobedience asks with a chuckle.

'Would you shut up!' Dragon roars at him.

Every ruler is dead silent.

'When you did not succeed, why didn't you wait for me before you do things your own way?' He gestures round. 'Can you imagine the damage you have caused?' No one speaks. 'I have told you many times that you just don't attack a giant. If you attack him and you fail, you make him stronger!' He looks round at them in frustration. 'With what you have done now, getting Brethren now is getting more and more difficult if not impossible.' There is another round of silence as he looks very thoughtful. 'I'll have to go to The Father in the courtroom and get a permission to send a dart of sickness at his wife.'

'What if you don't get it from him?' Doubt asks.

'I know how I can get it form him,' Dragon says with a wave of superiority. 'I have done it before. I did it to a Believer called Job, you remember him?'

'Yes,' they all says in different ways.

'What will you do if you get it?' Disobedience asks curiously.

'You can hold your peace for now,' Dragon says. 'When I get the permission, I'll come back and tell you what to do.'

Almost immediately, he returns to the courtroom with the case of Brethren.

The courtroom which is usually filled with elders from Eternity kingdom and a few members of council of rulers from kingdom of Doom. The representatives of each of these kingdoms are there only to represent the interests of their kingdoms.

'I am sorry for the interruption in the proceedings,' Dragons says to The Father, The Judge. 'I have to see what is happening in my kingdom. Comforter is making use of Brethren to wreck havoc into my kingdom.'

'Do you have a complaint about that?' The Father demands.

'Yes, your majesty,' Dragon says with a bow. 'The Redeemer, The Defense counselor of Believers gives more than enough powers to his people so as to do me such harm. To me, that's unfair.'

'Objection, Father,' The Redeemer says.

'Sustained,' The Father says.

'We have it in the constitution of Eternity that Believers that follow The Word has the host of Eternity behind him in everything he does.' The Redeemer says. 'If they command anything in my name, we are bound by the constitution to do it for them.'

'That makes it more unfair, Your Lordship,' Dragon tells The Redeemer. Of course, he knows that The Redeemer is so powerful that his name alone is enough to wipe out his entire kingdom. He knows further still that he cannot go beyond the limits that are set for him by The Father. This is the main reason he has to get permission before he carries out certain plans. Because of these limits, which he always wants to extend, he plays on the nature of The Father who is just and faithful to everyone even to Dragon his enemy. 'When small tempter like me is not given the fair chance to try certain Believers and let everyone see whether they deserve to inherit Eternity kingdom or not, it makes us feel that The Judge is being partial because The Redeemer is his son and Believers in question are his people.'

There is murmur in the courtroom. The representatives of kingdom of Doom say, 'that's true!' while the representatives of Eternity say, 'lies!'

The Father beckons on The Redeemer and whispers something into his ears. The Redeemer is expressionless as he nods with understanding.

'I grant you the permission to try him,' The Father says.

There are expressions of wonder on the faces of representatives of Eternity kingdom. The representatives of Doom give a cheer of joy and hail Dragon.

'We know Your Majesty is very just,' Dragon says, looking much happier than anyone.

With the permission to try Brethren, he leaves the courtroom and goes to pay him and his wife a personal visit.

CHAPTER NINE

Levity's name is changed by The Redeemer into Gentle, having been promoted into the level of a matured soldier that can tackle warriors of Dragon in the levels of principalities, power and even at times rulers of darkness. She seems to enjoy her new position in the hierarchy of soldiers of The Redeemer. She not only fights along side with her husband but also uses her weapon of warfare to pull down the stronghold of enemies of Believers. She is very fervent and diligent in reaching out to people for The Redeemer, creating lots and lots of enemies for Dragon. Before long, she has become mother of several thousands of people in The Spirit. When the rulers of darkness express their anxieties as she goes about freely, wrecking havoc in Doom kingdom, Dragon tells them to watch the way he is going to strike her and her husband.

Dragon enters Brethren's house without visible appearance, making it hard for Brethren or Gentle to notice him. His operation is made so sophisticated that when things begin to go wrong for Brethren, the giant does not know what is going on.

Dragon shoots the first deadly dart at Gentle. The dart catches her on her left breast. At first, she does not know she is been hit. When she begins to feel some pains, she goes to the hospital where the doctor says she is having a breast cancer.

'I'm a Believer,' she says to the doctor who is also Believer called Hope. She attends Brethren's Fellowship. 'The Redeemer can never allow this to happen to me.'

'Believers do fall sick, sister Gentle,' Hope says. 'Even if we fall sick, The Redeemer has made provision for us to be healed. The Word tells us that by the strokes of the whip on his body, we are healed. I've seen many people who are healed of more deadly diseases by The Redeemer. We, doctors only treat people but it is The Redeemer that heals.'

Gentle smiles at Hope and whispers, 'thank you, my sister. You have strengthened me with your words.'

'It's an honor to be used strengthen a great soldier like you,' Hope replies.

'What are we going to do now?' Gentle asks.

'I will give you some drugs to control the disease from growing. It will also relieve you of your pain. The drugs are quiet expensive but I'll see if I can buy you all you need for now.'

Gentle covers her face with her both palms and begins to sob.

Hope controls her emotion, stands up and goes to hug her. 'I can't explain why it is Believers that have to go through this but, as someone say it in a song, when we are gathered for our homes in Eternity kingdom, we shall understand it better. We shall tell the story how we overcome our enemies that are causing us much pains.'

Gentle smiled brightly. 'Thank you so much, my beloved sister. I see gains in the midst of pains. I feel joy in midst of depression. I feel the love of The Redeemer through you even when I feel so sick. The fact that someone like you can still lift me up when I'm down is enough for me to go back into the battlefield and lift up those who are wounded in The Flesh, The Spirit and The Mind.'

'No, my sister,' Hope says. 'I might have to put you on bed rest if I have to treat you. You've been hit with cancer. It can cost you your life if care is not taken.'

She signs. 'Okay.'

And so Gentle is hospitalized. Brethren is almost heartbroken when he discovers what is wrong with his wife but Comforter encourages him. Although his activities are reduced to some extent as he has to take time to look after his wife, he still manages to go about the business of The Redeemer.

He tells the rest of Believers at the meeting that he needs them to talk to The Redeemer about his wife. He says, 'I don't want to appear like a super man because I'm not. It is through the strength of Comforter that I can do all I'm doing. What my wife is going through is enough to make me lose concentration in the work but I know I'm the target of the enemies. So I want you to, please, rally round and help me in The spirit. I cannot fight the battle alone and I cannot afford to be tortured in The mind.'

Of course, nearly all Believers at the meeting give their huge support that encourages him. Even sister Flirt who is now addressed as sister Faith, having been promoted into the second level soldier of the Redeemer gives her full support. She makes herself available to sister Gentle and helps Brethren stands firm in The Spirit. She is constantly waiting on The Redeemer, talking to him that she will not eat until sister Gentle is on her feet. She cries to The Redeemer each time she is alone with him, thinking she is the cause of what Brethren and his wife are going through.

The Redeemer asks her when she is in The Spirit one day, having her quiet time with him, 'what my servant and his wife are going through has nothing to do with you. In fact I don't see anything you've done wrong.'

'I tried to tempt him to sleep with me, Lord,' Faith tells The Redeemer.

'When, how, where?'

'You mean you can't remember?' She is surprised.

'No,' the Redeemer says. 'Even if you do anything wrong, the moment you repent of it, it is wiped out from The Word. No one in Eternity or in The Spirit remembers anything that is not in the record. The Dragon cannot use it against you except you keep it in The Mind. Once you're forgiven, anything you have done wrong is forgotten. So cheer up, my daughter, and take your meal.'

'No, Lord, please,' she says. 'You have to do something about sister Gentle. We need her on her feet. We cannot afford to have her in that condition.'

'Not all decisions are given to my people to make. The reason is that they don't see beyond their immediate environment and situation. It's a torn in The Flesh, really, but my strength is enough for all of you.'

'When are you going to heal her?'

'At the appointed time, things would be put to rest.'

'What do you want me to do now?'

'Continue to do all Comforter is leading you to do,' he tells her. He pauses for a while before he adds. 'I have to say this to you: I'm proud of you.'

'You are prod of a wretch person like me?'

'I call you Faith. Don't give yourself the name I've not given you. Besides, you're no longer what you used to be. You're so matured now that I can count on you. I am going to make you a great soldier that will terrorize the enemy that is terrorizing my people.'

'What?!

'Yes, daughter,' The Redeemer says. 'I'm going to build you and you shall be built into great soldier.'

'I don't think I deserve that kind of position,' she says. 'I'm not worthy of you, let alone that position.'

'I make as many as believes in me worthy to be children of The Father. As for the position of a great soldier, with me all things are possible. You'll see what I mean when the time comes.'

After several other encounters with The Redeemer in The Spirit, Faith begins to grow so strong that she catches the attention of other Believers, including Brethren who marvels at her speedy growth. Of course, it is apparent to most of Believers that she is been having series of encounter with The Redeemer. She so fits into so many positions at the meeting, including Brethren's that Doom feels the impact of her activities. Gentle always feels very happy each time her husband tells her how Comforter is using Faith to make exploit for The Redeemer when he visits her in the hospital.

Gentle tries to get up from her sick bed when Faith visits her in her room one day, smiling, but she quickly and gently holds her back. 'You've not gotten the strength to move yet, mother,' Faith tells her.

Gentle smiles at her. The humble trait in her shows she had truly been meeting with The Redeemer. By placing herself in the position of her daughter, she can perceive it at once that she is broken down and remolded.

'You'll need to get up on your feet soonest,' Faith says, sitting on the chair that is close to her bed, 'because we need you to lead us in our quests for The Redeemer.'

'The Redeemer is never short of great soldiers, you know,' Gentle replies softly. 'If one is down, another one comes up again. I think you might have to replace me for now.'

'Oh, no,' Faith says, 'nobody can replace you.'

'You do realize that nobody is indispensable. Who would have thought that The Redeemer would raise you up to do the work at the meeting when I was hit?'

'There are few great soldiers like you, mother. I'm sure The Redeemer will never want to lose any. He would rather lose the slaves than to lose the soldiers that set them free with The Word just as a fisherman would rather lose the fish than to lose the net.'

Gentle smiles. She seems to be growing weaker everyday but everybody knows that she will soon be on her feet. She says quietly, 'your argument is sound and factual but it is not the truth. The truth is: we can never have enough soldiers. That's the reason we have to constantly tell The Redeemer to raise up great soldiers like you.'

'I really don't want you to consider me a great soldier because I give The Redeemer a lot of problems before he could have the whole of me.'

'Who didn't given The Redeemer problems anyway?' Gentle asks. 'I gave him lots of it. For instance, I almost let my husband fall when I denied him of what is rightful his.'

'I see,' Faith says, trying to forget what she tries to do to Brethren. 'I think your husband is a powerful giant in The Spirit. He knows when and how to take the battle in The Flesh into The Spirit because Comforter is always with him.'

'You're right, my sister,' Gentle says thoughtfully. 'I'm much blessed to have a husband like that.' She looks at her, smiling. 'I know The Redeemer would give you a husband like him.'

'How do you know, mother?' Faith asks curiously.

She shrugs. 'The Redeemer does not always give great strength to a woman and give little or no strength to her husband. It is either their strengths match or that of the husband is greater.'

'But I've seen cases where wife is greater.'

'The activities of the wife are always affected because the husband would not see things the way she sees them.'

Faith is thoughtful for a while before she says, 'you scare me, mother.'

'How?'

'I don't want my activities for The Redeemer to be tampered with by my husband but, with what you're saying, I might have to be very careful about my choice for marriage.'

'Actually, someone like you cannot afford to choose by herself because it can affect the battles with the enemies in The spirit, The Mind and even The Flesh. I've seen where marriages reduced great warriors into meat for the enemies to devour, destroying lives in all the battlefields. But I know The Redeemer cannot afford to let that be your case. It is better not to marry at all than to get involved in the marriage that can reduce your strength or ultimately destroy your chances of making it to Eternity kingdom.'

Faith nods. 'That's the courage I need, mother. I promise The Redeemer and you that I'll not marry outside the perfect will of The Father.'

'That's very good. You'll marry a giant that matches your strength in The Spirit.'

'If The Redeemer does not give me a giant as a husband, I'll not marry at all.'

'That's a very good decision but you know it is not an easy thing to do.'

Faith frowns. 'How do you mean, mother?'

Gentle smiles and says, 'as you know, Believers fight battles in The Spirit, The Mind and The Flesh. None of the battles in these areas is easy to overcome. Sometimes we get victories through the help of others just as you have come here to cheer me up. This role you're playing right now is designed by The Redeemer for you, not for my husband.' Her voice becomes quiet. 'The reason is that he is hit by what is happening to me. This makes him fights like a wounded lion. In other to encourage him to keep fighting, I have to pretend as if I'm comfortable. The truth is: I'm not comfortable in this kingdom.'

Tears blind Faith's eyes but seeing Gentle's smiles, she manages to smile. 'Father Brethren needs you, mother. That's the more reason you have to get up on your feet on time.'

'I'm willing but you know the wound has sucked up all my strength in The Flesh,' she whispers. 'If not for the fact that my husband needs me for now, I would have long requested The Redeemer to take me home. What is so agonizing is that I'm no longer useful to The Redeemer or to my husband. I lie down here on the sick bed, doing nothing while my husband is out there fighting the enemies that can bring him down through the weapons of The Flesh.'

'Mother,' Faith says quickly, holding her hand with both of hers, 'you talk as if you are ignorant of many things about your life. Your presence alone inspire so many people, let alone what you teach us. What you're sharing with me right now is a proof that you are still useful to The Redeemer. In essence, he is still using you to build other soldiers. What you call sick bed is made a pulpit and the hospital room is actually a lecture room for me to learn from you. Besides that, I know you've been talking to The Redeemer about us, asking him to give us victories in out quest to reach out to those are lost in this kingdom.'

Gentle draws her closer to herself, looking delighted. She cuddles her and whispers, 'thank you so much for making me feel relevant again. I love you.'

'I love you too, mother,' Faith whispers back to her.

After a brief silence, Faith withdraws and says, 'you were talking about the roles of others in our lives before we can get victories while addressing the issue of marriage.'

'Oh, yes,' Gentle says as if it just occurs to her to continue the discussion. 'The marriage of a Believer is very vital in his or her life. It can be a blessing if it is instituted according to the perfect will of The Redeemer or a curse if the believer is yoked in marriage with non-Believer or someone who pretends to be a Believer. Through the marriage of a Believer, children that would be future soldiers of The

Redeemer can be raised. Secondly, through the union of the couple, the husband and the wife can chase ten thousand of the enemies instead one chasing one thousand with the amour of war of Believers.'

Faith looks very thoughtful for a long time before she sighs. 'Your words are powerful, mother,' she says. 'I know you are talking from the experience an old time warrior but what I don't really understand here is that you had no biological child. What could have accounted for that?'

'That's a very good question,' Gentle says, smiling pleasantly at her. 'I had a child at the early stage of my marriage but I lost it when the pregnancy was seven months old. I had three miscarriages after that. The Dragon caused all these problems but The Redeemer made us understand that he permitted him to do that. We don't have to ask him why he allowed him to do a thing like that because, as his soldiers, we don't ask questions. It is enough that he let us know that he permitted it. But we do know that there are sacrifices to be made before we can find those who are lost in the kingdom of man. We have to endure pains before others can receive gains and there are battles to be fought on behalf others before they can get victories. This is how the life in Eternity kingdom is designed. The Redeemer has to strip himself of his eternal glory and power before he could come and help us fight the battle we cannot fight by ourselves. He became poor so that we can be rich with the gifts of The Father in Eternity, he died so that we can live. If The Redeemer can do all these for us, why should we hold anything back from him or why shouldn't we pay all the sacrifices he demands from us so that others can be blessed?'

After another long thoughtful silence, Faith unexpectedly bursts into emotional sobs.

Gentle looks startled, 'what's wrong, my beloved?'

Faith says in the midst of her tears, 'I can see why and how you broke down. You've gone through so much and you have made so much sacrifices for the good of others that I wonder if I can cover half of the journey you've gone through before I break down.'

'It's the grace I have from the Lord,' Gentle says in a weak voice. 'It's the cross I am always willing to carry till I meet The Redeemer in Eternity kingdom. If The Redeemer designs this kind of cross for you too, he will give you the grace to live through the journey.'

'Mother, you are a great soldier of The Redeemer,' Faith says, drying her tears. 'Is there any chance of being just like you, however small it may be?'

She smiles. 'Let me put it this way. I did not make myself like this and you did not make yourself. So let us remain whom The Redeemer had made us to be and strictly follow his orders, asking him to make his thoughts our thoughts and his will our wills. Through that we can consciously or unconsciously follows his way. And through following his way, we can carry out all the assignments he specifically gives to each of us.'

Faith holds her hand again, smiling. 'I thank you, mother. I'll never forget this moment for the rest of my life.'

Gentle cuddles her again.

CHAPTER TEN

The kingdom of Doom is getting restless as the battle against Brethren and his wife turns against them. Dragon hopes to strike Gentle with dart, ties her to the hospital bed with breast cancer and then make Brethren vulnerable to the attack of a principality warrior called Adultery. Flirt who is now called Faith goes through vigorous training at the feet of The Redeemer. Without knowing about this training, Dragon plans to use her again to pull Brethren down. But the plan seems to be falling apart as Faith fights along side with Brethren instead of making herself available as Dragon's tool. In fact, the activities of Faith nowadays are causing catastrophe in his kingdom. Many people he ordains to be with him in Doom when they leave kingdom of man are already changing their routes to Eternity kingdom through her operations in The Spirit! As if that is not bad enough, she is getting thoroughly equipped by The Redeemer to set free those he holds in bondage over the years. If he had known she is such a potential threat who is going to be picked by The Redeemer to terrorize him, he would have struck her dead when he had the chance.

Dragon holds a meeting with rulers of darkness who are busy fighting so many Believers as usual, instructing principalities to kill the babes in The Flesh and in The Spirit and telling warriors in the class of powers to terrorize and kill matured Believers in The mind. He wants to mandate the rulers of darkness to do all they can to reduce giants in The Spirit into midgets so that the least of his warriors can easily tackle them.

'We really have to do something about Brethren and Faith,' Dragon says dryly.

'Who is Faith, my lord?' Ignorance asks.

Dragon looks angrily at him. 'You really mean you don't know?'

'No, my lord,' he replies.

'Flirt had been changed to Faith when The Redeemer picked her

59

up where she is wounded in The Spirit. He healed and equipped her in The Spirit. She is almost as dangerous as Brethren and she is fast growing into a giant now.'

Every ruler at the meeting except Arrogance who is yet to admit that he has failed looks stunned.

'At first, we have Brethren fighting us with others like his wife whom we assumed as midgets. He feeds them with The Word that makes them grow into matured soldiers. His wife is also growing into giant. So I seek permission in courtroom to strike her with a dart. She's now down but now we have Faith coming up.'

'May be you shouldn't have struck Brethren's wife in the first place, my lord,' Arrogance says, trying to cover up his lapses.

'Brethren is the target, you fool!' Dragon roars at him.

'Perhaps we should have struck Brethren directly instead of going through his wife,' Prayerlessness says.

'If it's that easy,' Dragon says, looking at him, 'why didn't you do it? You had the chance to do it, didn't you?'

'It's Comforter that frustrates all my efforts, lord,' Prayerlessness says in defense, regretting saying a word.

'How?' Dragon wants to know.

'Brethren is always in The Spirit where he gets all his victories, my lord,' he replies. 'You know I often rely on others to bring our victims into The Flesh or The Mind before I can relatively strike them. But it's not easy for anyone of us to drag Brethren from The Spirit into The Flesh or The Mind.'

'Fine!' Dragon says with frustrating smiles. 'Everyone of you, especially you Arrogance!' He points at him. 'You must admit you're facing the same problem in striking Brethren. He knows we are trying to strike him but he's not striking back at us directly. Instead he is reaching out to our slaves, turning them against us and using Believers, including babes to strike us. Invariably, he is telling us that he is too big to deal with us directly. So he uses midgets to strike us. That's what I call insults with injuries!'

Now everyone knows Dragon is furious. They know further still that they are not supposed to say a word when he is mad.

They are all silent as Dragon expresses his frustrations and anger. No one can really say who he is angry at but they know he can transfer his aggression to anyone that gives him any reason to do that.

'Brethren's wife is bedridden because I want his demand of her womanhood to be so prolonged that it would be easy for us to use Flirt to bring him down. But the plan is not even close to execution before things fall apart. Flirt is no longer a sickly or dead Believer but a matured soldier of The Redeemer. Brethren's mind is so occupied by the condition of his wife and his works that he cannot think of a woman. But that's not to say hope is lost. Of course, you know the rule that we don't give up on anyone until he or she has gone to Eternity.'

'What's the hope?' Arrogance asks, hoping to make up for his lapses.

'That's a good question,' Dragon says, smiling for the first time. 'From what I gathered so far, Brethren loves his wife very much. If not that he loves The Redeemer much more, he would have abandoned the work completely and focused on his wife. I want all of you to think of straining Brethren's relationship with The Redeemer.'

'That's practically impossible!' Ignorance says, surprised that Dragon can bring up an idea like that.

'Ignorance, you better shut up and listen!' Dragon bellows at him.

Everybody is dead silence. Of course, they are all afraid of him and his crazy idea.

'Ignorance,' Dragon continues, 'you're going to cloud him in The Mind and makes him see the reality in The Flesh. When the sickness of his wife is prolonged after much efforts to bring her back to her feet, you will make him ask The Redeemer why his wife's sickness is so prolonged. I've gotten permission from The Father not to allow Comforter to interfere with this. The least The Redeemer can do is to take the woman to Eternity kingdom. I'm sure he's not ready to do that, at least not at this moment.

'When Ignorance opens his eyes to the reality in The Flesh, Prayerlessness will begin to lure him away from The Spirit. Indiscipline will use his warrior called Unguarded Thoughts to rope him in The Mind before bringing him to The Flesh. In case any of you have lost track of the routes in the three battlefields, let me explain it to you.' He brings out a map.

The rulers of darkness surround him as points at each of the locations on the map. He explains, 'this is Eternal Doom kingdom below the entire structure, where we are bringing the beast that will terrorize mankind and mark the people for total destruction after The Redeemer comes to take the real Believers to Eternity kingdom.

'Above Doom kingdom is the kingdom of man and at the highest location is Eternity kingdom. The locations of the three battlefields are here, here and there... Here is the route of The Flesh... It is a very broad, the easiest and the closest way to Eternal Doom. The Flesh is located somewhere between the kingdom of man and Eternal Doom.

61

No man can see the kingdoms of Doom and Eternity if he is in The Flesh. And anyone who cannot see the two kingdoms is vulnerable. It makes it easy for us to deceive and enslave the people at this location. We usually strike our victims and take them to Doom kingdom at this location since it is closer to us than it is closer to Eternity kingdom.

'The Mind is located a little bit above The Flesh where you can partially see Eternity kingdom and also see everything in kingdom of man and a small part of Doom kingdom. In The Spirit, however, you can see almost everything, including all the kingdoms. It's hard for us to defeat Believers that are fighting or walking in The Spirit but very easy for us to crush anyone that walks or fights in The Flesh. What we normally do to anyone in The Spirit is to lure him through The Mind and bring him to The Flesh where we usually kill him with spiritual death. If he is not revived in The Spirit before he leaves kingdom of man, he will end up in Doom kingdom.'

Dragon looks round at the rulers of darkness. Most of them already have the information he is sharing. He points at the location of the battlefield of The Spirit in the map. 'This is where Brethren, other giants and matured soldiers always walk and fight. They know what is going on in all the three kingdoms. They have The Word which serves so many purposes like the map of all the kingdoms, the light in the dark, the picture of The Redeemer, the solution to every problem and the answers to virtually all questions. The Word is also the sword to fight in The Spirit. More importantly, it is in The Spirit that Comforter usually takes Believers like John, Apostle Paul and a host of others to meet The Redeemer. It is in The Spirit that you will find the courtroom where I get permission to tackle Believers. Actually, there are so many things going on over there, which I don't even know! If only I know everything, I would never make plans that would fail.'

'Can't we place a spy that will monitor what is going one in The Spirit?' Prayerlessness asks, looking frustrated like the rest.

'A spy in The Spirit - you mean one spy?' Dragon sounds surprised he asks a foolish question like that.

'Yes, my lord - at least one.'

'You imbecile, we have millions of spies even right in the courtroom of The Father! They are doing all they can to get me information about what is happening there. Even then, when a Believer talks to The Redeemer in The Spirit, they don't even understand what he is saying let alone to gather any useful information through what he is saying. And that's not to talk of the confusing language they use in Eternity.' He pauses for a while before he signs and says, 'we do have one great advantage, however. Most people, including so many Believers are walking in The Flesh. That is one of the reasons it is easy for us to strike them as we like. The problem is: the moment any of them begins to walk in The Spirit, he starts growing into matured Believer and even giant. So we have to use everything the people can see, including flashy things to tie them in The Flesh. Those waking in The Spirit can be lured to The mind and from there to The Flesh. If we can do this to Brethren, we'll bring him down.'

'How can we be so sure it'll work?' Ignorance asks, trying to avoid any confrontation with terrorist Brethren or any of the giants that may crush him. Of course, he is always afraid of Believers that has The Word because he knows they can easily defeat him with it.

'You're telling me it wont work when we have not even tried it,' Dragon says, glaring at him.

Ignorance is silent. He does not want any further argument with Dragon.

'You're going after him first,' Dragon continues. 'As I told you, you will cloud his mind with reality and hide as much information as possible from him. Through that, you can pave way for others to bring him to The Flesh where we can strike him. Do you understand?'

'Yes, my lord,' Ignorance says, feeling at little nervous about the new plan.

CHAPTER ELEVEN

Brethren is alone in the room at night, not knowing what else to do. He has gone to The Redeemer in The Spirit several times with the case of his wife but he is so silent about it that he wonders what goes wrong. Thinking he has offended him which could have made him so distant from him, he constantly asks him to forgive him of whatever he has done wrong. When nothing seems to move the Lord to intervene in the case of his wife, he asks for help among other giants. He tearfully asks them to bring his wife to her feet again. Of course, the giants rally round him in The Spirit and talk to the Lord about it. Still nothing changes. Now he is getting weary and hurt. What weakens him most is his silence in this case even though he talks to him about other cases.

Ignorance sees his chance to cloud Brethren with reality in The Mind. He begins to speak to him in a gentle manner, making it difficult for him to identify it as the voice of an enemy. 'The Word seems to fail you even though it once worked for you. Gone are the days when you can claim the promises of The Redeemer to lay hands on those who are sick and they shall be healed.' Ignorance pauses for a while to allow him to react to that. He knows if he says more, he may discover him as an enemy.

'Yes,' Brethren whispers to himself. 'I ask my Lord to search and correct me if I've gone into error but he's so distant from me. He doesn't treat me like this. What's gone wrong?' He begins to cry like a baby.

'Lord, it's becoming hard to please you….' Brethren is not sure if that is his voice or not but he knows it is not Comforter's. Comforter always encourages instead of saying things that will weaken him. 'Comforter are you there?' Brethren asks. 'Please, talk to me. I'm confused.'

'Brethren,' Comforter says gently, 'consider the story of Job in

64

The Word.'

Brethren quickly reaches out for The Word.

Of course, Ignorance disappears from the room that moment, knowing fully well that he is about to crush him with the sword of The Spirit.

When Brethren reads the story of Job, he understands that Dragon must have gotten permission from The Father to strike his wife with cancer.

Then Comforter says, 'if you keep your sanity in The Spirit, you will survive in the ocean of insanity in The Mind and in The Flesh.'

For the first time since the sickness of his wife, Brethren understands what is going on in The Spirit. The knowledge gives him the strength to hang on until The Redeemer would heal his wife.

*   *   *   *   *

Gentle's condition seems to be deteriorating instead of improving. Hope has done everything she can do medically to heal the cancer, including operating the breast but it has spread to other areas. She and Faith are always by her side to encourage her. With the two strong soldiers by her sides to fend for her, Gentle is able to maintain positive attitude through out, asking nothing from The Redeemer except the grace to carry the cross with joy.

Comforter takes her to meet The Redeemer in The Spirit where she is told that she should get ready to go home in Eternity kingdom. She becomes so joyous that day. She tells Hope she would like to go out of the hospital and talk to people about The Redeemer.

Hope frowns at her and says, 'you're too weak to do that. I can't allow you to go anywhere. I'm sorry.'

'Please,' Gentle pleads.

'No, please.'

'How about talking to the patients in the hospital?' she ask with a plea.

'I or sister Faith will do it for you.'

'I'll like to do it myself, please,' she pleads again. 'Even if it's just one person. I want keep doing what the Lord says even if I'm dying.'

Hope frowns at her, looking reluctant and wondering at her. She knows she is one great warrior that can be misunderstood easily.

'It means so much to me,' she says.

'Okay,' Hope replies reluctantly. She arranges with one of the nurses to take her round the patients.

Gentle goes from one ward to another to meet the patients, telling them briefly about The Redeemer. She tells them about Eternity and Doom kingdoms, pleading with them to accept The Redeemer as their Lord. She is able to reach out to eight people who become Believers that day.

In the afternoon, while Gentle is on her bed, resting, there is gentle wind that passes through the window. She opens her eyes and looks at the wall in front of her. There is a large opening in the wall with hosts of Angels, lining up on two sides. The lines reach up to Eternity kingdom. It is so glorious that Gentle cannot comprehend it. The Redeemer walks in between Angels, smiling at her.

'My lord!' Gentle cries with excitement.

The Redeemer stands in front of her and says, 'I would have sent Angels to bring you home in Eternity kingdom but I know your husband will stop them. So I decided to come to you by myself and ask you if you'll like to go home with me.'

'Yes, of course, my Lord!'

'Come on then. Let's go, my daughter.'

Two Angels help her change her mortal cloth that is made with dust into an immortal clothing that is white and glorious. Gentle appears so glorious and magnificent. That moment, she realizes that the wounds, pains, sickness, sorrows and all sorts of ugly things are actually the characteristics of the mortal cloths which everybody must wear if he or she is so live in the kingdom of man.

Leaving the mortal cloth on the sick bed in the hospital, Gentle follows The Redeemer to Eternity kingdom.

Hope is the first to discover that Gentle has gone to Eternity kingdom when she examines her mortal cloths on the bed. She rushes to her offices, locks herself up and begins to sob hysterically, saying, 'why, Lord? After all we did, you still take her away. We talked to you about her case. We fasted... Why, Lord?'

After crying for some time, Comforter speaks to her. 'Hope, the lives of all Believers are stories written by The Father, characterized by The Redeemer and directed by me. The Father has written it that Gentle has completed her assignment in the kingdom of man. She's gone to Eternity kingdom to rest. Someone had been prepared to continue her role.'

She takes a deep breath after Comforter speaks to her, dries her and goes back to see Gentle's mortal cloth again. Then she send a message to Brethren who just returns from the assignment The Redeemer gives to him. He is planning to go and see his wife in hospital when he gets the message that his wife has gone to Eternity kingdom.

Brethren reads the message and smiles. He does not believe it because he knows The Redeemer can never do a thing like that to him. When he gets to the hospital, however, he discovers that Gentle had actually gone home. He goes to where her mortal cloth lays and cries out in a loud voice, 'Gentle, I command you in the name of The Redeemer, come back!' He is silence. Nothing happens. Then he says in a whisper, 'my Lord, I know you can hear me. I have faithfully fought to expand the kingdom of The Father. I have gone through a lot in the hands of the enemies because of you. If I am indeed your servant, bring back my wife because I need her.'

The gate of Eternity is already opened for the Redeemer as he leads Gentle to the much talked about kingdom of The Father. The entrance alone and the joyful welcome which is given to Gentle is enough to make her forget where she is coming from.

Of course, The Redeemer hears Brethren's voice. He knows it is going to be difficult to make Brethren understands the plans of The Father. So he looks at Gentle who looks radiant with unspeakable joy and says, 'daughter you have to go back to the kingdom of man.'

Gentle looks puzzled. 'Why?'

'I have one last assignment for you.'

'Lord, I don't want to go back there. There are people you can send at the place.'

'Only you can do this for me.'

'Okay, Lord. What do you want me to do?'

'I want you to go back and inform your husband, my servant that it's you that decides to follow me.'

'I can't do this alone. Let's go together, Lord.'

'Oh, no,' he replies. 'If Brethren sees me in the kingdom, he will follow me by all means.'

'He loves you that much?' Gentle asks him.

He nods with smiles. 'I love him too - very much. You can tell him that. I would have loved to bring him home too but I still need him in the kingdom of man. There is so much to do for me.'

'What else do you want me to tell him, Lord?'

'Tell him what you see in Eternity kingdom and tell him someone had been prepared to take your place in his life.'

'Would you give me the privilege to know the woman, my Lord?'

Gentle asks.

'I know you're going to tell him,' he says. 'She is the woman that look after you when you're hit by Dragon.'

'There are two women in particular that really fend for me. Which of them?'

'Hope.'

'That's great, my Lord?' Gentle says. 'How about Faith, my Lord? Do you have plans to give her a giant as a husband?'

'You already promised her on my behalf that she'll marry a giant. So she's going to marry the giant that leads her to me.'

'Thanks, Lord. Eternity is full of secrets and mysteries.'

'Only the ones that are revealed to men are for men,' The Redeemer says. 'You can go to him now. He's waiting for you to come back. An Angel will lead you there and bring you back. I'll wait for you here.'

She bows. 'Yes, my Lord.'

CHAPTER TWELVE

Hope looks tearfully at Brethren who is sitting beside the bed with Gentle's mortal cloth, still expecting her to return from Eternity or to see The Redeemer. It is either he sees his wife back in the kingdom of man or he sees The Redeemer. He hopes to see the Lord anyway. If he is the one that comes, nothing can stop him from going with him. After all, what again will keep him in the kingdom of man that is full of pains and sorrows. The kingdom had been so ravaged by Dragon that he can hardly see anything good inside. Ever since he becomes a matured Believer, the only joy he has is that of the Lord, finding no place for comfort except in The Spirit.

'She is gone home, sir,' Hope says quietly. 'We have to pack her mortal cloth.'

'No, Doctor!' The voice does not sound like his. 'I never bargain this with the Lord.'

'The Lord gives and he takes,' she says in a whisper. 'Let her go in your heart.'

'Please, leave us alone,' he says. 'If she doesn't come back and I don't see The Redeemer, then I am not his servant.'

'Okay, sir,' she says gently and leaves the room, closing the door behind her.

After a while, Brethren perceives the presence of the messenger from Eternity though he cannot see him. He smiles and says, 'Lord, it's you I want to see.'

'Just then,' Gentle enters her mortal cloth again and sneezes.

Brethren laughs so loudly that Hope who is waiting outside hears his voice. She bursts into the room and looks so shocked to see Gentle back in her mortal cloths that she is speechless.

He looks at Hope and says, 'I told you the Lord will hear me, didn't I? Hallelujah! He has never fail me!'

Gentle begins to cry hysterically, feeling the pains of her mortal cloth all over again.

'You're welcome back, honey.' Brethren says.

'I've not come to stay, my love,' Gentle says within her sobs.

He looks stunned. 'why not?

'The Redeemer gives me one last assignment. He wants me to persuade you to let me go.'

He smiles ruefully. 'I wonder how you are going to do that?'

She unbuttons the top of her dress and shows him the part of her chest that has no breast. 'Is this what you marry?'

'You know it doesn't matter to me. In fact, that makes you more of a jewel, not only to me but to The Redeemer because you lost it while you were fighting along side with me to push the enemies back. Honey, you need a stronger persuasion than that.'

Gentle sobs so much that Hope slips on the floor and begins to sob too, burying her face between her laps. 'It's a great honor to be your wife and to fight along side with you in the battle,' she cries.

'No, honey,' he replies. 'It's a great honor to have you as my wife because I know the pains and the challenges of being my wife. You lost children and suffered persecution because of your position as my wife...'

'I ...didn't suffer all that because I'm your wife. I suffered that because I'm a warrior of The Redeemer.'

'That's the more reason I can't let you go. I need you, honey! Can't you see that? You inspire and give me strength when I'm weak. When everybody forsook me in the battlefields, you are the one that stood by me. Even on your sick bed, you tried to protect me. You almost asked me to make love to you when you are sick because you are aware I can be struck with the weapon of The Flesh.'

'Honey, my mission is over,' she says in a very weak voice. 'I have to beg you in the name of The Redeemer to let me go.'

'No, darling,' he says. 'I can't survive all I'm going through without you. Where in the whole kingdom of man am I supposed to get a woman like you?'

Gentle slowly points at Hope whose face is still buried between her laps, lost in emotional sobs. She whispers so that she wont hear her. 'The Redeemer says she's to replace me in your life.'

'That's a joke, you know,' he says. 'I wont buy that.'

'Would you rather have a bedridden wife that will be a liability to you or you'll let me go back to the glorious city in Eternity kingdom and rest. I've been there. It's very beautiful. Although you've talked about

70

the place several times but there's no way you can comprehend the beauty of that place.' She is smiling now. 'There is no pain, no sorrow nothing but bliss. The moment anyone steps into the place, he forgets where he's coming from. Oh, how I wish you know how Eternity kingdom looks like. If you know, you wont call me back here or try to make me stay. Love…' She hold his hand.

He grasps it with his both hands. He begins to sob as if he will tear his heart.

'If you truly love me, you'll let me go. The Lord wants me to get your permission before I go back to him in Eternity. He's sent an Angel that will take me back.' She smiles at him after a while. 'Would you let me go, my love?'

He nods slowly, still shedding tears.

'The Lord says if he comes by himself, you'll do all you can to follow him.'

He smiles faintly and dries his tears. 'I was hoping he'll be the one to show up. If he does, I'll definitely follow him. I can't find anything worth while in this kingdom again.'

'He says he needs you to rescue people from the enemies.'

'Yes, I know,' he replies. 'It's the assignment that keeps me in this kingdom otherwise I'll be long gone.'

'There are so few giants in the kingdom of man,' Gentle says. 'I'm so blessed to be married to one of them.'

'Whatever I am or whatever I do is not my making, you know.'

'I know, honey,' she says. 'What makes you different from most Believers is that you're ready to pay any price just to please The Redeemer.'

'Anyone who knows The Redeemer well enough will know that he deserves everything.'

'That's my giant husband talking.' Gentle smiles. 'The Lord wants me to tell you that he loves you much more that you can comprehend.'

'I know,' he says, beginning to sob again.

There is silence. Angel beckons on Gentle that it is time to go.

She looks at her husband. 'It's hard to say good bye but I have to go back now.'

'Can we spend few more minutes together?' he asks.

'The Lord is waiting for me at the gate of Eternity.'

'Okay,' he says reluctantly.

'Wont you kiss me good night?' She asks him.

He kisses her on the lips and says, 'god night, darling.'

'Good night, my love. We'll meet in Eternity,' Gentle says.

He nods.

With her last breath, she adds in a whisper, 'I'll be waiting for you in Eternity. Do all you can to get as many people down there because the place is glorious.'

Then Angel takes her back to The Redeemer in Eternity.

Brethren dries his eyes after a while and then stands up. He looks at Hope who now stands by the door. Her pretty and youthful face looks pale and gentle. He knows all she has done to keep his wife in the kingdom. He is also aware of the huge amount of money she has spent, spending much time with her to give her hope.

'Do you want us to pack her mortal cloth now?' She asks quietly.

'Yes,' he replies gently.

'Do you want me to send you a male nurse who can help you at home?'

'No thanks,' he says. 'I'll be fine. I just need time to be alone with the Lord.'

'Can I come and see you when I close from work?' she asks, feeling very concerned for him with no apparent reason.

He looks deep into her eyes. He can read great virtues in her face. 'Apart from my wife that goes home now, you're the most loving and caring person I've ever known.'

'I don't know why you're saying this,' she says. 'I just want you to be fine.'

'I know,' he says. 'I say this because it's not enough to just say: "thank you" for all you've done for my wife. Your labour of love will never be in vain. I can assure you of that.'

Then he leaves the hospital. When other Believers at his meetings hear the news, most of them, especially Faith are heartbroken although there are talks before then that The Redeemer may eventually take Gentle to Eternity. During the time Gentle's mortal cloth is committed to the dust, Brethren consoles the people, telling them a few things that happened when he first hears that she is gone home.

'I wanted to go with her,' he tells the Believers who are there as the dust is committed to dust and ashes to ashes. 'I talked to the Lord about it. I wanted him to come and take me home too because I cannot find anything worth living for in this kingdom. I said The Redeemer should either come and take me home too or he returns my wife.' He smiles, looking round at the people. There are so many of them. There are all very attentive. 'My wife came back from Eternity.' He pauses.

He can almost sense the disbelief among some of them. 'If you believe in The Redeemer,' he says, 'all things are possible. That assurance is in The Word.' He points at Hope. 'That loving and lovely sister who was her doctor was there when she came back.' Many of them look at Hope. 'Is it true or not, sister Hope?'

Hope stands up slowly from where she sits and says, 'It is true, sir. Since my years of experience as a doctor, nothing like that has ever happened.'

'Thank you, doctor,' he says.

Hope sits down again.

'She came back, she told me that she has not come to stay,' he continues, 'but rather to get my permission to go home. There is something glorious about her exit from this kingdom. I want to point that out in The Word in Revelation 21:4 where we are told that The Father shall wipe away all tears from our eyes, and there shall be no more death, sorrow, crying or pains for the former things are passed away.

'My wife was a great warrior of The Redeemer but she told me that her mission in this kingdom is over. She says she'll wait for me in Eternity because she knows nothing can take that glorious place from me. She said something very important which is what actually makes me address you on this occasion. She said I have talked about Eternity kingdom many times but there is no way I can comprehend the glory in that place. She said that the moment a Believer gets to the entrance of the city of Eternity kingdom, he forgets where his is coming from. According to what she told me before she went back finally, The Redeemer was waiting for her to take her to her mansion. So while we are saying goodbye to her in the kingdom of man, the host of Eternity kingdom are saying to her, "welcome home!"

'You're going to see her again if you remain a Believer till the day of your exit from this kingdom. She told me that when I'm going home, I should not come alone. I must bring as many people as possible. Eternity kingdom is a place we must possess with everything we have just like the story of a man who bought a field of precious stones in The Word. This man, as you know, sold everything he has just to possess the field. You must give away everything that can hinder you in getting to Eternity kingdom. I want to round up with the song my wife and I composed together while we were going through numerous trying periods.' He pauses for a while before he begins to sing:

Don't loss sight of The Redeemer

73

No matter what you're going through
Don't forget about Eternity
Even if all is well with you
Don't lose sight of The Redeemer

Don't lose sight of The Redeemer
Even if the battle is getting hot
Life here is a great battle
But the Lord will see you through
Don't lost sight of the Redeemer

Don't lose sight of The Redeemer
For without him, we are all dead
The end of life here begins with another
Don't lose sight of The Redeemer

Don't lose sight of The Redeemer
No matter what comes your way
No matter what you have given up
Don't ever give up The Redeemer
Don't lose sight of The Redeemer

Everybody present at the occasion are touched. They all stand up and give Brethren a big round of applause.

CHAPTER THIRTEEN

The information at Dragon's disposal makes him so confused that he is silent for a while, looking deeply carried away from the meeting he is having with the rulers of darkness. He wonders at the way The Redeemer is handling the situation. He does not expect him to take Brethren's wife to Eternity just like that, making him to wonder what he is up to. If he knows his plans, he will know how to frustrate it but he does not have the slightest idea of what he is about to do.

He sighs, thinking more deeply. He must think of what The Redeemer plans to do before he knows how else to frustrate it. With Brethren's activities so far, he is growing more uncontrollably dangerous everyday.

He has to stop all his activities or at the very least hinder him from moving forward. The battle of Eternal Doom against Eternity kingdom of The Father over the kingdom of man is getting to the point that, with few more giants like Brethren, destruction of everything he has been building for several thousands of years is inevitable. What gives him and his warriors great advantages are the legal ground which is given to him to control the kingdom of man and the power which The Father gives to man to choose between the right and the wrong ways. This power places man in the position to choose between whom to follow - The Redeemer who will never enforce his will over anyone or Dragon, who is an expert in deceiving and cajoling people into following his way. Apart from wrapping themselves in various forms and pretending at times to be soldiers of The Redeemer and even Angels of light, Dragon and the rulers of darkness know how to ensnare Believers through baits like materialism and sexual attractions. But the moment a person knows the truth, he will be set free. Once he is free, he becomes a problem unless the soldiers of Dragon do something about his growth.

The growth of a Believer is so crucial to The Redeemer that he pampers him at the infant stage. If, however, the Believer does not grow, he starts dying in The Spirit. That is the reason at least a matured Believer is placed around babe Believer to care for him. Even if he grows but does not produce, The Redeemer is always so disappointed that he cuts him off from his people and left to be on his own. Once he is on his own, he becomes meat for the kingdom of Doom.

The Redeemer relies on Believers to be productive by reaching out to slaves and set them free with The Word. Through that, he can have more soldiers that will launch constant and steady attack against kingdom of Doom whose warriors are determined to destroy the people.

'What does The Redeemer has in mind before he takes Gentle to Eternity?' Dragon asks aloud. He is not actually addressing anyone in particular because he does not expect anyone of them to know.

'I heard of a replacement,' Compromise says.

Dragon looks at him with interest. He is a little surprised he has some information though he is aware that Compromise always go extra mile to strike Believers.

'What's your source of information?' Dragon asks.

'I've been hanging around Brethren, my lord,' Compromise explains. 'I look for opportunity to open doors for other warriors to strike him since he's proving difficult to handle.'

'I see,' Dragon says thoughtfully. He looks at Ignorance. 'I remember I gave you an assignment like that.'

'My lord,' Ignorance says at once, 'I reported back to you that I can't get near him because he is always having The Word with him. The Word is too deadly for me to withstand. So I have to stay away from him.'

Dragon looks at Compromise. 'Perhaps I should have given you the assignment in the first place. You seem to be the only one who can dare The Word. So let's hear you.'

'I was with Brethren when he recalled his wife from Eternity kingdom of The Father soon after The Redeemer takes her away. She told him that The Redeemer is replacing her with someone else.'

'Who might that be?' Dragon asks quickly.

'Hope, my lord.'

Dragon frowns. 'Hope? Who is Hope?'

'She is one of the silent warriors of The Redeemer that stayed put with Gentle when you struck her with the dart of sickness.'

Dragon looks very thoughtful for a while, wondering at The

Redeemer again. He expects him to replace Brethren's wife with at least a matured Believer like Faith. Picking someone that is not even known to be dangerous makes him wonder again. 'What does this Hope weighs in our scale anyway?' He asks involuntarily.

'She carries a lot of fire, my lord,' Compromise says. 'In fact, she is the one that helps to sustain the strength of Brethren and his wife.'

'You mean she strengthens warriors?' Dragon looks a little puzzled like the rest.

'Yes, my lord. '

'How come we don't even know her?'

'She operates silently and secretly in her closet,' Compromise replies. 'She is always in The spirit, getting energy for warriors.'

'What!' Dragon springs up. 'How do you know this?'

'It's when I heard that The Redeemer has selected her to replace Brethren's wife that I checked on her. I was surprised too when I discovered this. Because she is always fighting us behind someone in The Spirit, we don't always see her around and because we don't see her, level one of our warriors are the ones dealing with her. The case is like asking a Principality warrior to fight a giant.'

'I see,' Dragon says thoughtfully. 'I wonder how many Believers we have underrated like that. There must be millions of them out there. I can see that this is one of the secret ways The Redeemer trains his soldiers. That explains how a babe Believer today can grow into matured one within some months.' He nods with understanding. 'We are not going to leave any stone unturned. We are going to combine our forces and deal with every genuine Believers as if we are dealing with matured ones or giants, no matter their levels. Through that we can destroy potential soldiers or giants of The Redeemer.

'We are going to take the battle into Believer's meeting ground.' He looks at Disunity, 'I want you to make use of the same old trick to divide and rule them, make them turn against each other.'

'Yes, my lord,' Disunity says at once.

Dragon looks at Ignorance. 'You must make babe Believers think they have the knowledge and the skill of matured Believers. You must influence them to fight with our warriors in the classes of powers and even rulers of darkness. By fighting our warriors that are above their strengths, they tend to lose the battle easily. Let the matured Believers think they are giants that can combat the rulers of darkness directly without the help of other Believers. Do not give matured Believers or giants rooms to fight us in pairs or groups by hiding the fact that they need each other before can get victories in the Battle.'

77

'Yes, my lord,' Ignorance says.

Dragon looks at Arrogance. 'You must go after both matured Believers and the giants. Make them to be full of themselves to the extent of paving way for Pride to go before their inevitable destruction.'

'Yes, my lord,' Arrogance replies.

Dragon gives one assignment or the other to the rest of the rulers of darkness. Before he tells Compromise what to do about Brethren's case, he says to everyone of them, 'the hope of all the people in this kingdom lies in the hands of Believers who are save and equipped with The Word. The Father or The Redeemer would not send Angels from Eternity kingdom to fight for the people even though they would be much more effective if they are directly involved in the battle. Because man lost his kingdom to us by breaking the law of dominion, man must be the one to fight us. There is no way he can fight us without the whole amour which The Redeemer gives only to Believers. Invariably, the people would need to be redeemed first, following the law of redemption before they can match the strengths of even the smallest of our warriors. The law of redemption establishes it that the belief of the people in The Redeemer and their deeds are essential ingredients before they become true Believers. Even if a Believer believes in The Redeemer, that is not enough. We believe too, don't we? That's the reason we tremble at the name of The Redeemer. Believers must prove what they believe by working for it. Because of this law, The Redeemer has to gather his soldiers among Believers. And before he can build them, he needs their co-operations by asking them to submit their powers of will and choice to him. We must ensure that the people are not built into soldiers by making them to keep their powers of will and choice. We will let the people enslave themselves with the powers, using them to destroy themselves. One of the best way to do that is to make them feel they own their lives and they can run it as they like. We will hide the fact that true freedom is when they submit their powers of will and choices to The Redeemer. This is easy for us to do because the entire mankind is blind. Nobody can see beyond his immediate environment, let alone to understand what is going on in The Spirit. We must ensure that the people remain blind by cutting them away from The Redeemer. The moment anyone of them meets The Redeemer, his eyes will be opened to what is happening in The Spirit. Once he knows what is happening there, he will start giving us constant problems like Brethren...'

He looks round at them before he ask, 'do you understand what I am saying here?'

They all nod.

'Now,' he says, looking at Compromise. 'The special assignment I have for you is to tackle giants. I want you to make Brethren compromise with the plan of The Redeemer.'

'How, my lord?' Compromise asks.

'If Hope is designed by The Redeemer to replace Brethren's wife,' Dragon says, 'you can be sure it is against our interest. So you need to manipulate the plan. Let someone else take that place. If someone who is not designed to occupy that important position in his life is placed there, he's bound to have problems. Through that mistake, we can strike him or make him weak or ineffective in all his activities.'

The rulers darkness give Dragon a big round of applause for the brilliant idea. Shortly after that, the meeting ends.

CHAPTER FOURTEEN

Brethren is always alone in The Spirit, waiting for hours to hear the voice of the Redeemer. Comforter lifts him up to the place through a bus that is known as Praise And Worship. He always enter the bus alone or with other people whenever he going into The Spirit while Comforter lifts the bus up. He has been going to The spirit more constantly since his wife left for Eternity kingdom, making it a little hard for people like Hope and Faith to communicate with him. He seems to enjoy staying in The Spirit, waiting on the Lord or communicating with Comforter but the people, especially in his congregation are becoming concerned about his condition in The Mind. Whenever he is in The Spirit, they often assume he is in The Mind where he is vulnerable to the dart of loneliness, past memories and even high blood pressure.

Being a medical doctor, Hope assumes he is going through a lot in The Mind. So she tries to look after him by giving him some drugs that will relieve him of whatever he is going though. Instead of Brethren taking the drugs, he will retrieve to The Spirit, waiting on the Lord. Before long, he has grown more slim than his natural size.

While he is sharing The Word one day, the people; especially Faith and Hope conclude that he really needs a woman in his life. He makes it obvious to them that he is getting fed up with the life in the kingdom of man.

'The kingdom of man have turned into fierce battlefields,' Brethren says when he is sharing The Word. 'The only way we can survive it is to focus our attention on Eternity kingdom. The passion to possess the place must be evidenced in our lives if we are really serious about getting to the place. This is the reason The Redeemer says that the kingdom of Eternity surfers violence and violent people take it by force. In other words, you must fight your way to Eternity kingdom with the whole armour of war.' He pauses for a while.

80

'I've had to give up a lot of things to be in this shape. The Lord takes away a very precious thing from me for the reason best known to him. I must admit that what The Redeemer has taken from me is taking its toll on me...' He falls silence suddenly and then continues after a while. 'I need you to keep lifting me up in The Spirit because I'm sick and tired of what is happening in this kingdom. I want to go home but the Lord says to me. "You still have a lot of battles to fight. You still have people to reach with The Word. You still have people to train and you still have babes to feed." Much had been given to me and much is expected from me. I have to justify the investments of The Redeemer in me by performing all the assignments he gives me before I go home.

'I remember how the Lord picked me up when I was in the mud like a pig. He washed me with his precious blood at a place called Calvary. He gave me the Eternal Being called Comforter. He equipped me with The Word, using some giants to build me into his soldier. Many of these giants have gone to Eternity kingdom today. I am expected to be productive like the giants of old. It would be a crime if I'm not productive because if I'm not, I have wasted Eternal investments. The Lord cannot tolerate me or anyone who is not productive. That's why he says in The Word that anyone that is not productive will be cut off and thrown into Eternal Doom where he will turn into meat for the enemies.'

Brethren's sharing for that day reflects the state of his mind. It proves to everyone that he needs a woman who will be by his side, giving him reasons to fight on and a reason to stay fit.

Faith goes to see him at home that day to point out a few things to him. Sitting opposite each other she says, 'we've been talking to The Redeemer about you.'

'I know,' he says quietly.

'The way you shared The Word today confirms what the Lord says to us.'

He looks at her with interest, 'what did he say?'

'You need someone by your side,' she says.

He looks thoughtful for a while before he nods slightly.

'The Word says can two walk together unless they agree? If they are able to walk together after agreement, while one is chasing one thousand of the enemies, the two will chase ten thousand if they come together as one.'

Again, he nods with agreement.

'I think you have to give another woman a chance your life.'

81

'Okay,' he says.

She stands up. 'That's all I've got to tell you, sir.'

'Thank you, sister Faith,' he says, standing to see her off. 'I must admit that my vision is a little blur in The Spirit for now. Please, let me know whatever the Lord tells you.'

She hesitates for a while, briefly recalling what Gentle has shared with her shortly before she went to Eternity kingdom. She can almost hear her quiet voice addressing her.

'... Actually, someone like you cannot afford to choose by herself because it can affect the battles with the enemies in The spirit, The Mind and even The Flesh. I've seen where marriages reduced great warriors into meat for the enemies to devour, destroying lives in all the battlefields. But I know The Redeemer cannot afford to let that be your case. It is better not to marry at all than to get involved in the marriage that can reduce your strength or ultimately destroy your chances of making it to Eternity kingdom.'

'That's the courage I need, mother. I promise The Redeemer and you that I'll not marry outside the perfect will of The Father.'

'That's very good. You'll marry a giant that matches your strength in The Spirit.'

'If The Redeemer does not give me a giant as a husband, I'll not marry at all.'

'That's a very good decision but you know it is not an easy thing to do.'

'How do you mean, mother?'

'As you know, Believers fight battles in The Spirit, The Mind and The Flesh. None of the battles in these areas is easy to overcome. Sometimes we get victories through the help of others just as you have come here to cheer me up. This role you're playing right now is designed by The Redeemer for you, not for my husband. The reason is that he is hit by what is happening to me. This makes him fights like a wounded lion. In other to encourage him to keep fighting, I have to pretend as if I'm comfortable. The truth is: I'm not comfortable in this kingdom.'

Faith is moved emotionally as she recalls the conversation she had with Gentle.

Brethren notes the sudden change in her expressions as she shrugs and says, 'it is well.'

'You seem to have something on your mind,' he says, looking at her expectantly.

'Yes,' she says reluctantly. 'It has to do with the dialogue I had with mother Gentle. I'm not sure I'm in the position to tell you.'

'I told you my vison is blur. So I need people like you to give me information that will be of use to me. Please, tell me whatever it is.'

'Mother told me when she was hit and tied to the hospital that she has to pretend she was comfortable just to encourage you to keep pushing the enemies from the fold of The Redeemer.' Her voice turns into a whisper as she adds, 'She said you fight like a wounded lion. Now that she is gone, I think you fight like a sickly giant. Only a woman in the position of your wife can bring you back to shape. This observation may not be from the Lord. It's my observation.'

Brethren looks thoughtful for while, thinking of what Gentle told him about Hope being the person The Redeemer plans as his new wife. He is not sure if she was talking to him out of great love she has for Hope. He looks at Faith and asks, 'did she tell you who this woman might be?'

Faith hesitates for a while before she says, 'she did not tell me directly but she gave me a hint of whom the woman might be.'

'Who?' Brethren asks eagerly.

She shakes head slowly, indicating her desire not to tell him. 'You have to find that out yourself because it is a decision that is personal to you. Besides, I don't think it's proper for me to tell you because I'm involved.'

'Please, tell me. I'm pleading with you,' he says. 'It may be in line with what I'm thinking.'

'I think the woman you're going to marry is closer to you than you think,' she says slowly.

'You are still coding the message. Please, tell me specifically who.'

'That's for you to discover, sir,' she says. 'The woman could be waiting for you to tell her.'

He recalls the details of what Gentle tells him when she returns from Eternity before she finally lives.

'... Honey, my mission is over. I have to beg you in the name of The Redeemer to let me go.'

'No, darling. I can't survive all I'm going through without you. Where in the whole kingdom of man am I supposed to get a woman like you?'

Gentle slowly points at Hope whose face is still buried between her laps, lost in emotional sobs. She whispers so that she would not hear her. 'The Redeemer says she's to replace me in your life.'

'That's a joke, you know,' he says. 'I wont buy that.'

'Would you rather have a bedridden wife that will be a liability to you or you'll let me go back to the glorious city in Eternity kingdom and rest. I've been there. It's very beautiful. Although you've talked about the place several times but there's no way you can comprehend the beauty of that place... There is no pain, no sorrow nothing but bliss. The moment anyone steps into the place, he forgets where he's coming from. Oh, how I wish you know how Eternity kingdom looks like. If you know, you wont call me back here or try to make me stay. Love...'

Without giving Faith a hint of what is going on in his mind, Brethren concludes that Hope may be the one that is intended by The Lord to take the place of his wife. Even though it seems hard to believe, with what Faith is saying, he might have to tell Hope what Gentle says and find out if the Lord tells her the same thing.

Few days later, Brethren goes to see Hope in her apartment. She is thrilled to have him as a guest. She tries to treat him specially but he objects to it. He tells her he comes for a discussion.

After offering him soft drinks which he accepts with appreciation, they sit opposite each other to talk.

He clears his throat before he says, 'first of all, I have to thank The Redeemer for your life. You're a real blessing to me and to so many other people.' He sighs to take a sip from the soft drink. 'I want to know why you are still single if you don't mind telling me.'

'I'll tell you, sir,' she says politely. 'Well, I'm not quite single.'

He looks puzzled. 'How do you mean?'

She smiles and says, 'I'm engaged with a brother who attends another Fellowship.'

He looks more puzzled. 'You're what?'

'I'm engaged to a doctor like me, sir,' she says. 'Is there anything wrong in that?'

'Oh, no, no,' he says quickly, trying to hide his confusion. 'I... just wonder if he's the will of the Lord for you.'

'Of course, he is,' she says quickly. 'He's a very wonderful Believer like you and good soldier of the Lord.'

'That's not the point sister Hope,' he says quickly before she is carried away by what attracts her in the man. 'The question is how you know he is the will of the Lord for you?'

'I talked to the Lord about him and I feel it in The Mind when I was meditating in The Word that he's the one he has for me.'

'I see,' he says slowly, wondering if Gentle is the one that misunderstands The Redeemer for saying Hope is to replace her or

Hope is the one missing the way. 'Did the Lord tells you in The Spirit anything about the man?' He asks her.

She looks reluctant as she replies. 'I'm not so sure.'

'Did the Lord tells you anything about me?'

'Yes,' she says. 'Comforter told me that a woman had been prepared to replace your wife when she first left for Eternity.'

'I see. Who is the person?'

'I don't know - really,' she replies, 'but I think it's sister Faith.'

'Actually, I'm not asking of an opinion. I want to know what the Lord tells you specifically because I cannot afford to compromise with the will of The Redeemer in the area of marriage. The obvious reason is that marriage can become an extra heavy cross for a Believer to bear if it is not instituted according to the perfect will of The Redeemer.'

'Well, sir,' Hope says. 'To be on the safe side, I would say I don't know?'

He asks gently, 'are you sure you don't know?'

She frowns at him, a proof that the idea of getting married to him never crosses her mind. 'I wonder why or how you expect me to know anything about the woman that is chosen for you by The Redeemer.'

He is in dilemma. He is not sure whether or not to tell her the last words of Gentle about her becoming his wife. Telling her without her getting confirmation from the Lord may seem like taking advantage of her love for him and his wife. If he does not to tell her, however, he may be hiding from her vital information that may help her to make right decision about her marriage.

As if reading his mind, she asks, 'is there anything I'm supposed to know which I don't know, sir?'

Although he is yet to decide whether to give her the information or not but when asks for it, he knows he must take the to risk of telling her. He says, 'when my wife returns from Eternity kingdom the second time, she told me The Redeemer says you're the one that is prepared to replace her in my life.'

Again she frowns, looking more confused. After a while, the confusion changes into smiles. 'Well, sir, I guess she probably expressed her desire.'

'Under that circumstances,' he insists, 'she couldn't have said what the Lord did not say. More so, she knew how delicate the issue of marriage is.'

She is thoughtful for a while before she says, 'if I don't know you to be a giant in the Lord, I would have doubted this. I don't doubt you. I'm just confused. Actually I am not prepare for this. So I have to talk to

85

the Lord about this.'

'Yes, you have to,' he says. 'None of us can afford to dabble into an issue like this without being sure this is what the Lord wants.'

She nods, still looking puzzled. 'Even if it is the will of the Lord, a lot of questions have to be addressed. First, how do I withdraw my word which I have given to the man I wanted to marry, my family and his people?'

'You've gone that far?' He asks, a little surprise.

She nods ruefully.

He shrugs. 'To me, what's important is what The Redeemer says. If what you say is contrary to what he says, you have to withdraw from it. After all, wrong choices are some of the things our enemies can use to fight against us. You my be misunderstood at the initial stage for following instructions of the Lord but at the end, you'll overcome your critics with good results.' He stands up to go. 'I guess you have the duty to talk to the Lord about this and let me know of your decision to marry me or not.'

Hope looks at him with wonder. 'You're proposing to marry me just like that?'

'Just like that, sister,' he says. 'Unless you feel there is a protocol I must follow, that's a proposal. You're free to accept or reject it. But I'm convinced the Lord wants me to marry you.'

'You do realize, sir, that you're dealing with a weak person, considering your strength.'

He smiles. 'I'm flattered,' he says. 'I'm not dealing with a weak person. I'm dealing with a warrior who fights behind warriors. If you think the enemies do not see you, you're missing the point.'

'Why me?' She asks in whisper.

'If you know how many times I've had to ask myself a question like that, you'll know I don't have the answer. The Word is the only thing in the position to answer the question. Go to the Lord in The Spirit. He will answer all your questions.'

'Did he answer you when you ask him the question?' She asks him gently.

'Yes,' he replies. His answer is either "I love you" or "I need you for the assignment".' He is silent for a while. 'I have to go now.'

'Can we talk a little more, please?'

'We'll talk again some other time.'

Again there is silence as she walks him to the door. They pause on the way to look at each other's eyes. There is something from Eternity that appears on their faces.

'What do I see on your face now?' She asks him quietly.

'I see it also on your face.'

'What's it?'

He smiles, opens the door and leaves without saying a word more.

Comforter whispers into her ears. 'It's name is Love Divine.'

CHAPTER FIFTEEN

Faith is always under pressure to let Brethren know what she feels as the will of The Redeemer. She gives him a hint when last she sees him but he seems not to understand. Perhaps he needs to confirm from the Lord that she is the one who is prepared to be his wife. With his level of understanding of The Word and the operation of Comforter, she expects him to know who is to be his wife.

She goes to him in another day to continue the discussion about the issue of his wife from where she stops.

After a brief exchange of pleasantries, she comments that he appears to be getting over his emotion.

He replies, saying, 'yes, thanks to the Lord for sending you to let me see the cause of my low spirit.'

'So you get the message after all,' she says.

'Yes,' he answers innocently, not having the slightest clue of what she is having in mind.

'You appear to have gotten solution to it.'

'Yes, I have. I have to give another woman the chance to be my wife, as you said. That is the solution.'

Faith smiles, thinking he is about to propose to her to be his wife. 'Is this woman aware of the important role she's about to play in your life?' She asks cautiously.

'Yes,' he says, completely oblivious of her thoughts.

'Who?' She asks with greater caution.

'I'll like to keep that a secret if you don't mind,' he tells her in a very polite manner.

'You just confirmed to me that the Lord used me to address the problem…'

'Yes, yes… but…'

'You don't trust me?' She sounds disappointed.

'Oh, no, not that I don't trust you.'

'If you trust me, then tell me who.'

'The person is Sister Hope,' he replies slowly.

She frowns. 'Sister Hope? How come?'

Brethren looks a bit puzzled, wondering what she means. 'Is she not good enough to replace my wife?'

'Oh, no, not that,' she says quickly, trying to erase the impression that she is against his choice. 'She's very good actually but she told me at one time that she's engaged to one Brother Frivolous who attends Carefree Assembly. He's also doctor like her.'

'I see,' he says quietly and thoughtfully. 'But I think she's the one The Redeemer has prepared to replace my wife.'

'I don't want to question the source of your conviction,' she says, 'but you must realize that there are three or four sources of information of which only one is through Comforter. The rest are from Dragon or his warriors in Eternal Doom and through The Flesh or The mind.'

'I know all these,' he says.

'Of course, I know you know,' she says. 'In fact I learn this from you but hear what the book of Isaiah says in The Word in Chapter 42 Verse 19 and 20,' she takes the book with the title: "The Holy Bible" and opens to the passage, reading, "who is blind but my servant, or deaf as my messenger whom I send? Who is blind as he who is perfect, And blind as the Lord's servant? Seeing many things, but you do not observe; opening the ears, but he does not hear.'

Brethren looks thoughtful as he meditates on the passage. Then he asks, 'what do you want me to understand now?'

'Well,' Faith replies, 'I just want you to know that the servant of The Redeemer can also be blindfolded by cloud of thoughts that are not in line with the will of the Lord.'

There is a brief thoughtful silence before he says, 'you seem to know something I don't know.'

'I'm not in the position to tell you anything, sir.'

'Even after admitting to you that I don't have all the facts?' He says. It is more of a question than a statement.

'You have a duty to go to the Lord and find out the fact,' she says. 'I'm almost sure that the Lord cannot tell you to marry someone in marriage courtship.'

'Why do you think so?' He asks quickly. 'Marriage courtship is not marriage. So it can be broken.'

'You're saying a vow can be broken?'

'Well, yes, if it's not in line with the will of the Lord,' he replies. 'Even covenant can be broken.'

89

'Really?' She appears to be hearing that for the first time.

'Yes,' he says. 'Only The Redeemer is bound by his words. Once he says it, it's going to be.'

'Are you so sure it is the will of the Lord for you to marry Sister Hope?'

He hesitates for a while. 'Somehow,' he says.

'You don't appear sure.'

'I'm almost sure though not so sure.'

'Has it been confirmed to her or anyone?'

'Somehow, it has been confirmed.'

'There are too much uncertainties in all you're saying, sir,' she says. 'You can't based your decision about your choice for marriage on assumptions or uncertainties. There is too much at stake here. You know that, sir, don't you?'

He looks thoughtful for a while, nods slowly. It appears his ability to see in The Spirit is getting weaker. Yes, Faith is right to think he, the servant of the Lord is getting blind. Perhaps he needs to ask her what she knows as the will the Lord in the area of his marriage. Since he trust her, he can rely on her ability to see better than him.

He asks suddenly, 'tell me whom you know as the choice of The Redeemer for me.'

'I'm not in the position to tell you that, sir,' she says, 'even if I know the person.'

Compromise who is the one manipulating the whole scenario requests Dragon's help when it is getting to the time Brethren will make crucial decision.

Dragon transforms himself into Comforter, making Brethren feel that The Redeemer is about to deliver him the message.

'Brethren,' Dragon says exactly in the gentle way Comforter normally addresses him, 'Faith is the one prepared to replace your wife. That is what I have sent her to tell you.'

'But,' Brethren says in The mind without making a sound, closing his eyes, 'my wife says Sister Hope is the one The Redeemer has prepared for me.'

'She is only influenced by all the care she has received through her.'

'I saw Love Divine in Sister Hope's eyes,' he says, 'and she sees him in my eyes too, which confirms we are meant for each other.'

'That's not Love Divine. It's lust, Brethren,' Dragon says. 'How can you love someone who is engaged to someone else. With the strength of Hope, you should know that she couldn't have gone into

90

such relationship without The Redeemer getting involved.'

'I hope this not manipulation,' Brethren says.

'You know this is not manipulation,' Dragon says. 'Faith as you know is a stronger soldier of The Redeemer, far stronger than Hope. You need a strong soldier like her, not Hope who is just coming up. That is the reason I let Faith does all she is doing while your wife was on sick bed.'

'I see…' Brethren is convinced and he falls for it. He says, 'let your will be done, oh Lord.'

Dragon disappears immediately after that, leaving Compromise behind to put finishing touches to the plan to mislead Brethren into marrying Faith.

'Sister Faith,' Brethren says after a long silence that indicates to her that he is communicating with Comforter. 'I think I now know the person the Lord has for me.'

'Who?' She asks slowly.

'I think you don't want to tell me because it is you.'

Faith drops her stare and sighs. At last, she says to herself, her dream is coming true.

'You should have told me before now,' he says. 'You would have saved me the trouble of going to propose to marry Sister Hope and also the pain of going to break up with her.'

'I'm sorry but I don't think it is proper for me to do that,' she replies. 'The Word says that he that finds a wife finds a good thing, not she that finds a husband. So it's for you to find this out.'

'I don't find anything wrong if you tell me,' he says, 'especially when I confess to you what is happening to my vision in The Spirit. If you have not aided me in this matter, I would have gone for Sister Hope, believe me.'

'I thank the Lord for helping you to know the person,' she says.

'But let me ask you,' Brethren says. 'How do you know I'm the one the Lord has chosen for you?'

She sighs, looking thoughtful. 'First mother Gentle told me that the Lord would give me someone like you. I made a promise to her and The Redeemer that day that I would not marry anyone except a giant Believer.' She pauses, looking thoughtful as she recalls what she sees in The Spirit while sleeping. 'Secondly, the Lord confirms it to me while sleeping. I saw the two of us in The Spirit getting married in one assembly. Although the man I married in The Spirit is you in everything but your attitudes are different a little.'

'Why do you think there's difference in the attitudes?' He asks.

'Well,' she replies, 'I don't really know but I guess the Lord wants to alter your personalty a little bit.'

'Why do you think he'll do a thing like that?' He asks, laughing.

'I guess he wants us to fit into each other's life.' She laughs with him. 'I've always desire a giant who has gentle personalties and that of a great soldier.'

'Really?' He asks, looking interested. 'What is my own personality if I may ask.'

'You're a no nonsense giant!'

He burst into a prolonged laughter.

Seeing him laugh for so long, she laughs with him, feeling happy.

'I think you're going to make me happy,' he says. 'I didn't know you have this sense of humor.'

'You're going to make me happy too.'

Meanwhile Hope constantly reflects what Brethren tells her about marrying him and his conviction which is the basis of her own conviction. Evidenced with Love Divine they see in each other's eyes, she concludes in her mind that The Redeemer really plans them to be married. As a Believer, having made the decision to marry Brethren, she goes to meet Brother Frivolous who at the initial stage is not serious about getting married. It is what he notices in her that influences him to proposed to her for marriage which she accepts after taking little time to think about it. She does not seriously consult The Redeemer before she accepts his proposal. In fact, she just had a serious talk with the Lord about her marriage when Brethren proposes to her. She meets the Lord in The Spirit who tells him that it is his will that she marries Brethren. He, however, warns her of the impending problem that will put into a test the trust she has in him in this issue. As a first step, he instructs her to break up with Frivolous, which she is trying to carry out.

She goes to Frivolous the day she talks with the Lord. His house is locked when she gets there but she perceives he is inside. After knocking at the door persistently, he eventually opens it.

'What are you doing inside since?' She asks him.

'Well... em... I'm sorry,' he says. 'I'm kind of busy.'

'You're busy doing what?' She asks, wondering.

'Since I say I'm sorry,' he replies, a little irritated. 'I expect you to be satisfied with that.'

Comforter says to Hope in a whisper, 'he is having a visitor.'

'Who's your visitor?' Hope asks suddenly.

'A visitor?' He asks with a frown. 'Who tells you I have a visitor?'

'Some close to me.'

'Who is the person?'

'Is it true or not?'

'Don't answer any question with a question,' he says.

With the way he is acting, Hope knows he is truly having a visitor. Then she puts one and two things together and concludes that Frivolous is probably under the attack of Fornication. The thought that he is probably overcome by a warrior of Dragon in the class of principalities indicates to her that she cannot be equally yoked with a man like that in marriage.

'The only way to prove that the person is telling the truth or not,' she says, 'is to let me look around.'

'If you don't find anyone, what would you do?'

'I will apologize.'

'That's not enough,' he says in a harsh tone. 'You'll tell me who tells you I'm having a visitor.'

'Okay,' she says, 'and if I find anyone in here - a female especially, our relationship ends here.'

'Okay,' he replies. 'Suit yourself.'

She looks around but to her surprise, she cannot find anyone. It is apparent that the person is either hiding somewhere or has sneaked through the back door while he engages her in a dialogue. She, however, goes to the kitchen door that leads outside and finds the door opened.

'I usually leave that door open,' he says when she opens the door, looking at him for explanations.

'Well, doctor,' she says politely, 'we have to hang our relationship in one place until I verify some things.'

Then she leaves the house.

Frivolous later goes to challenge Hope's colleagues who know about his affairs with another lady for poking noses into his business.

'What did I do?' One of colleagues that is challenged asks.

'You went to tell my fiancée that I'm having an affair with someone.'

'How can I?' he demands. 'After all, you told me she's just your friend when I asked you about your relationship with her. By the way, is Doctor Hope really your fiancée?'

'That's none of your business.' Frivolous says, leaving the office angrily.

Later the colleague tells Hope how Frivolous comes to challenge him, forcing him to tell her about the lady that sometimes to go to his house.

That instant moment, Hope decides to put an end to her relationship with Frivolous. She looks forward to develop a deep relationship that will end in marriage with Brethren.

CHAPTER SIXTEEN

Dragon again holds a meeting with the rulers of darkness to discuss the case of Brethren and other Believers that are troubling their kingdom.

'So far, my lord,' Compromise says, 'we've been able to manipulate the will of The Redeemer in the choice of Brethren in the area of marriage.'

Dragon does not look very impressed as he says, 'if Faith were to be an unbeliever or a nearly dead or sickly Believer like Frivolous who is intended to be yoked with Hope, getting Brethren down would be so easy. But she is not. This makes me wonder if we'll be able to strike Brethren the way we want even if they are yoked in marriage.'

'We will be able to get him down,' Arrogance says, 'if we are able to use other people against him.'

'How?' Dragon looks interested.

'With the information we have about Faith,' Disobedience says, 'she can easily break the rules in The Word if she is frustrated. Indiscipline can use his warriors like High Level Provocation or Frustration to work her up. She does not have the stamina to handle any of these warriors, going by our record. That is what makes her far from being a giant. Even if we are not able to get Brethren down for whatever reason, we can easily make him ineffective in the battle against us if he is yoked with Faith.'

'You think Brethren is that easy to handle?' Ignorance asks. 'We've made series of fantastic plans to bring him down since our scale declared him a giant but we are unable to execute any of them.'

'Ignorance,' Dragon says with irritation, 'you obviously know little or nothing about this issue. So keep your mouth shut. Just because you have failed does not mean others will.' He looks at Indiscipline. 'What can you say about Faith? High Level Provocation and Frustration are parts of your warriors. What do you have to say with regards to what Disobedience says?'

'My Lord, Disobedience only borrowed the warriors from me at one time.'

Dragon glares at him. 'You mean you never use valuable warriors like that?'

'I have, my Lord,' Indiscipline says, 'but not when dealing with a super giant like Brethren.'

'What makes you think he's supper giant?' Arrogant demands.

'We know that, don't we?' Indiscipline replies Arrogance.

Dragon says, 'there's nothing like supper giant in the kingdom of man. Even the so-called-giants are so few that you can count them.'

'Well, I'm sorry, my lord,' Indiscipline says. 'I've tried several times to use some of my warriors against giants like Brethren, I and my team are no match for them.'

'Well, we are trying to yoke Faith with Brethren in marriage. If you can't get him directly, you have her to work on.'

'Okay, my lord,' Indiscipline says, 'but you need to first yoke them together in marriage before I can come in here.'

'We are almost through with the plan to yoke them together,' Dragon says. 'When we succeed, the rest of the job is yours. You're to use Provocations, Frustrations, Intolerance, Annoyance and all the warriors you need to first bring her down. When you bring her down, he will become vulnerable. I'm certain that The Redeemer does not plan to yoke them together because her weakness can make him vulnerable to our attack. Now that we are able to come up with a good plan, let's move on with it. We cannot afford to waste any more time.' He looks at Compromise. 'You can go and yoke them together as fast as you can before Comforter interfere with our new plans.'

'Yes, my lord,' Compromise says.

A moment later, the meeting ends and each of them goes about his mission which is either to steal the people in the kingdom of man or to kill the Believers in The Spirit or to destroy all of them altogether in Doom kingdom.

No one knows exactly what is happening as Faith goes about to announce her courtship with Brethren to everyone. When Hope hears about it, she pays Brethren a visit in his house.

Brethren feels guilty because he is yet to know how to announce to her that he has confirmed it through Comforter that The Redeemer does not plan them to be married. He, however, makes her feel at home when she comes for a visit. 'What can I offer you, doctor?' He asks.

She smiles and shakes her head silently. 'Nothing, sir. Thanks.'
'Oh come on....'

'I'm fine,' she says. 'I've only come to confirm what Sister Faith said about your courtship with her.'

He gesticulates aimlessly, looking more guilty as he sits apposite her. 'Well, em... Actually, I don't know how to say this,' he says gently, 'but I... em... I don't think it's the will of the Lord... em… we ….. em....'

'It is not the will of the Lord that you and I get married. Is that what you're trying to says?'

He cannot look at her eyes as he whispers, 'yes'

'Look at me in the face, giant, and say that again,' she says in a shaky voice.

He still cannot bring himself to look at her.

She is really crying in the inside. Her voice continues to shake with emotion as she says, 'I believe you can recall what you told me and what I told you when you came to see me at home.'

He steals a glance at her and looks away again. The feeling of guilt is growing out of his control.

'I will refresh your memory, sir, if you don't mind,' she says in a whisper. 'I was alone when you came to me. You told me what Sister Gentle said after she returned from Eternity. You told me she said The Redeemer plans that I am to replace her in your life. Is that not what you said?'

He nods without saying a word.

'I told you I believe you because I know you are a giant who knows what he is doing. After the Lord gives me good reasons, I break up my relationship with Brother Frivolous,' she says.

'You broke your relationship with him?' He asks, looking at her briefly.

'Yes,' she whispers, 'but that's not the issue. The issue is not even me or you either. The issue is about the will of the Lord. Comforter made me see that Brother Frivolous is not someone I can be equally yoked with.'

'Didn't you know this before I came to you?' He asks quietly.

'No,' she says. 'Let's not dwell on that because that is not, again, the issue. The issue here is the will of the Lord.' She pauses briefly before she continues, 'the day you proposed to me, I saw Love Divine in your eyes and you saw it in mine. That is all I need as confirmation before I decided I would marry you. It was that day I realized that I have made a mistake about my choice but you said something, which I must repeat to you as good counsel. You said that wrong choices are

97

some of the things our enemies can use to fight against us. We may be misunderstood at the initial stage for following instructions of the Lord but at the end, we will overcome your critics with good results.

'As you know, we all need Comforter as guidance in all we do otherwise we'll go astray.'

'Yes,' he whispers. 'But Comforter told me Sister Faith is the one the Lord plans for me as my wife.'

She smiles because she can almost sense it that he is blindfolded by powerful warriors of Dragon. She concludes that if a giant like Brethren can be blindfolded, all Believers are vulnerable to the manipulation of Dragon. 'Have you honestly and seriously taken this matter to the Lord in The spirit?'

'Yes,' he answers.

'And you are sure going into marriage with Sister Faith is the will of the Lord for you?'

'Yes,' he answers though he looks uncertain.

'Then Sister Gentle did not really hears what The Redeemer says about my role in your life.'

Just then, Faith knocks at the door and comes in. She cheerfully greets Hope but Brethren is lost in his thoughts, reflecting the last moments he had with Gentle before she finally goes to Eternity.

Brethren can almost see himself in the hospital with Gentle sobbing on the bed while Hope slipping on the floor, weeping as well. Gentle is saying, 'It's a great honour to be your wife.'

'No, honey, it's a great honour to have you as my wife.

'My mission is over lover, can't you see that?'

'No, darling, I can't survive without you. Where in the whole kingdom am I supposed to get a woman like you?'

Pointing at Hope, she says, 'The Redeemer says she's to replace me in your life...'

Before Brethren knows it, his eyes are filled with tears. The two ladies who are still exchanging pleasantries look puzzled when they see his tears.

'What's the matter, love?' Faith asks.

Brethren dries his tears, looking a little embarrassed and says, 'Sister Faith, would you, please, excuse me and Sister Hope for a moment? We are in the middle of a very important discussion before you came in.'

Disobedience who is as invisible as most of Dragon's warriors stands behind Faith and says, 'you're not going to let him get rid of you and let Hope get him back, are you?'

'What is it you want to talk about that I cannot hear?' She demands sternly.

'It's personal,' he replies.

'What's so personal that will leave me out of the discussion between the two of you? After all you've proposed to marry me and I've accepted.'

'Yes, I know,' he says. 'But remember I told you I proposed to Sister Hope first.'

High Provocation and Frustration begin to work on Faith almost immediately, revealing her weakness to the rest. 'So you've been keeping two ladies as your fiancées?'

'You know that's not true.'

'You just confirm it now that you proposed to marry two women,' she says. 'The whole world must hear this.'

Hope who hates conflicts, especially between two soldiers of The Redeemer stands up to go. 'I think I need to take my leave now.'

'Where do you think you are going?' Faith asks with Frustration by her side. 'You think you can cause problem between me and my fiancé and go away just like that.'

'Ask him what I told him,' Hope says gently though she is surprised that Faith seems not matured enough to handle Provocation and Frustration that are obviously pushing her to misbehave, 'I didn't tell him anything except to remind him of what he told me.'

'What did he tell you?' Faith asks harshly.

Hope points at him. 'You can hear it directly from him and leave me out of this, please.' She leaves the house hurriedly before Faith has the time to reply.

After a while, Faith calms down and goes to sit close to Brethren, but he pulls away to sit apposite her. She sighs before she says, 'please, love, don't let the enemy come between us.'

'I wonder who is the enemy in this case,' he says indifferently. Hope has gently removed the blindfold in his eyes by simply refreshing his memory about the discussion he had with Gentle, his gentle wife.

'When I say enemy,' Faith says, 'I don't mean her. I mean Dragon or his warriors.'

'You know, Sister Faith,' he says, 'I just noticed that you have one weakness. You don't know how to handle Provocation and Frustration. That weakness is enough to ruin all the works I and my wife had been building over the years if I give you the position of my wife.'

'I'm sorry,' she says quietly. 'I can work on that.'

'Well, until then, I don't want you to tell anyone again that we're in marriage courtship. I'm suspending that until I hear directly and convincingly from The Redeemer of his will for my life.'

Faith almost flares up but she manages to hold back Frustration that is about to hit her again, knowing fully well that her overreaction will only make things worse.

'I want you too to go to the Lord in The Spirit and to talk to him about his will for you,' he says. 'He may have me or someone else in mind for you. I know this one thing for sure: if I'm the one for you, no one can take me from you. If, however, I'm meant for Sister Hope, no one, not even can take me from her. The reason is that the Lord is the one who closes the door which no one can open. He opens the door which no one can close. Once you have this at the back of your mind, you will not try to resist his will or plans.' He pauses for a while to study her expressions.

She looks thoughtful, wondering if she is wrong to think Brethren is the will of the Lord for her or not. She asks him, 'you suspect I may not be the one the Lord choose for you?'

'I don't want to work by assumptions or opinions,' he says. 'Even if you are the one for me, I still want to know the type of will it is.'

'How do you mean, sir?'

'Well,' he says, beginning to explain. 'There are basically three types of wills of the Lord. We have the perfect will which is the best for all Believers, especially those who want to attain and maintain the status of matured Believers or giants till they get to Eternity kingdom. It is not just perfect for all warriors of The Redeemers but also very vital. The reason is that it makes easy for the Lord to make best use of their potentials and helps reach the peak in endeavours in this kingdom. Besides that, it will ensure steady victories in the battle against the warriors of Dragon.'

'Next to that is good will of the Lord. This type of will is good but not good enough. If you are operating within the good will of the Lord, you'll not reach half of the height you're supposed to reach because your potentials can never be maximized.

'The third will is the most disastrous of all the wills. It is called the permissive will of the Lord. This type of will is the one you obtain from the Lord by force. Because the Lord will never enforce his own will on anyone, he permits some impatient or disobedient Believers to have their ways with whatever they want to do. Anyone operating within this type of will is dinning with Dragon or his warriors. They can easily knock him off and reduce him into meat for consumption.

'As a soldier of The Redeemer, we must operate under the perfect will of the Lord. Do you understand my points?'

She nods slowly and thoughtfully.

CHAPTER SEVENTEEN

Dragon is really restless now as he holds meetings with the rulers of darkness, again discussing about the plans to bring Brethren down.

Everyone at the meeting can see it clearly that the plan to yoke Faith with Brethren in marriage instead of Hope is beginning to fail. They are beginning to see that Brethren is graduating into a greater threat. It appears that he needs little or no help from other people before he can get back on track whenever he is missing the way. With what they try in vain to do to him so far, it is apparent to Dragon and all the rulers of darkness that there is no way they can reduce him or stop him from fighting with the full powers of a giant Believer, let alone to bring him down.

Dragon thinks the least they can do to him right now is to sling mud at him and ruin his reputation as a giant Believer. Through that, a lot of Believers he trains in the battle can fall in The Flesh and in The Mind. With Provocations and Frustrations who are already working on Faith, if warriors like Rumours and Backbiting is given the assignments to aid them in scandalizing him, he can be really hurt in all the battlefields. Backbiting will continue to bit him at the back until Discouragement is invited to take him into oblivion, where he will be ineffective in the battle against them. Once he is ineffective in the battle, The Redeemer will be forced to take him to Eternity kingdom. Through that again, they would have succeeded in getting rid of one of the major threats in the kingdom of man.

'Yes!' Dragon says aloud, looking excited.

The rulers of darkness look at him with interests. Some of them guess at once that he is coming up with a fresh idea while the rest like Disobedience, Arrogance, Indiscipline, Compromise and a host of others who fail to bring Brethren down wonder when Dragon will give up the fight against him.

'If after having gone this far,' Dragon says, looking round at them, 'Brethren still waxes stronger, it would be a crime to give him up. The kingdom of man belongs to us!' There is a tone of anger in his voice. 'We'll do everything to protect it against the likes of Brethren.'

'My lord,' Compromise says quietly as if he is afraid of the repercussion of what he is about to say, 'you always say at this meeting that if we strike our victims and fail to bring them down, we only make them stronger. I believe you. We have made Brethren a terror in our kingdom by striking and failing to get him down all the time.'

'Yes, that's true,' Disobedience says.

'What's your point now?' Dragon asks impatiently.

Compromise looks hesitant to speak again when he sees the expressions his face.

'Talk to me, warrior!' Dragon bangs the table.

Quietly, Compromise says, 'I think it's about time we relax a little bit.'

'Relax and give him the chance to ruin our kingdoms right before our eyes!' Dragon roars so loudly that everyone at the meeting is shaken. 'Do you have any idea of what you're trying to say? You want us to leave Brethren alone and allow him to lead our slaves to The Redeemer who will readily use them to fight against us? Aside from that, have you forgotten that this war is not a battle between us and the kingdom of man but the kingdom of Eternity. I have told you here that The Redeemer cannot send his soldiers from Eternity to fight us because it is man that gives us the legal ground to take over his kingdom. So The Redeemer has to redeem man from us and use as many as believe in him in the war against us. And you...!' He points at Compromise. 'You're telling us to give up in this battle and allow soldiers of The Redeemer like Brethren to make soldiers out of our own slaves! You're insane! Now tell me and everyone here that you're insane!'

'I am insane!' Compromise says quickly before he bounces on him with full force.

'Listen, everyone,' Dragon says, looking round at them, 'and listen for your own good. Anytime we sit down here to talk about how to tackle any soldier of The Redeemer and I hear any talk about giving up on anyone, I'm going to tear you into shreds. Do you understand me?'

'Yes, lord,' the rulers of darkness says in unison.

'Now back to the business,' Dragon says after a brief pause. 'With what has happened so far now, we cannot yoke Faith together

103

with Brethren in marriage. I'm certain Comforter is the cause of all the mess in our plans. In any case, we still have a chance to strike Brethren through my new plans.' He looks at Disunity. 'It's your turn to strike again, ' he tells him.

Disunity bows and says, 'I'm ready, my lord.'

'You have Malice as one of your warriors, right?'

He nods. 'Yes.'

'You can enlist Rumour and Backbiting from the army of Indiscipline and carry out the assignment against Brethren,' Dragon says, looking thoughtful as he recalls the details of his new plan. 'You'll send Rumours and Backbiting to scandalize Brethren that he is dating two women. Rumour and Backbiting will spread the news that he is sleeping with the women at different times. You'll use Provocations and Frustrations that are still holding Faith in bondage to pave way for Malice and Pride. Through the operations of these warriors, Faith will feel the need to defend her dignity after having been jilted by Brethren. Faith will be influenced by Malice and Pride to scandalize Brethren. If you are able to do all these, even if Brethren is not hurt as I expect, we would have reduced Faith into a midget or babe Believer that can be handled by warriors in the class of Principalities. Not only that, many people Brethren is leading in the fight against us will turn against him or fight against those who supports him. With this kind of division, we can easily bring the battle from The Spirit to The Flesh where we can easily bring down many matured Believers or reduce them into midgets.'

The rulers of darkness are so dazed by the brilliant idea that they hail Dragon, shouting, 'hail, our king!'

The rulers of darkness soon begins to implement their plans against Brethren and other Believers.

Provocations and Frustrations are the first set to go into action, working on Faith who becomes embittered that she is jilted by Brethren. Malice begins to disarm her of her armour of war. Instead of thinking of the perfect will of The Redeemer as Brethren teaches her, she is feeling humiliated. Provocations and Frustrations keep talking to her at different times in The Mind. 'How are you going to face the people you have informed about your courtship with Brethren when they hear that he is not going to marry you?' Frustrations says.

'Can you imagine the pain and the humiliation?' Provocations says.

'What am I going to do now?' Faith asks herself.

'You need to defend your dignity. For you to do that, you must let the people know that Brethren proposed to marry the two of you at the same time,' Pride suggests in a gentle voice, 'other wise people would think that you try to lure him into marriage. You remember the time you try to lure him to bed. He could have told his new lover, Hope. She in turn will tell other Believers. Then everybody will think you're the one that try to lure him into marriage just as you try to lure him to bed.'

Faith feels more bitter as she admits to herself, 'this is true!'

'Then you have to strike him by telling everybody how irresponsible he is before he paints you into a prostitute that is desperate to get married to him by all means,' Malice says.

'Yes,' Faith says, getting furious and frustrated for no apparent reason.

She begins to tell everyone that is close to her how Brethren proposed to her and Hope at the same time, hiding the whole truth and adding a few lies to make up for the truths. Because she is also a matured Believers, virtually everyone that hears her story believes her. Before anyone knows it, Brethren and even Hope had become a subject of discussions that are usually characterized by Rumours and Backbiting. Soon, Brethren who is once respected by most Believers begin to look down at him as an Hypocrite. Since Rumours and Backbiting have sophisticated means of hiding vital information from their victims, Brethren and Hope do not know the damage they have done to their reputation until the day he announces to the people their plan to get married.

One of the Believers called Brother Critics stands up at the meeting and asks boldly, 'are you planning to marry two women, Giant Brethren?'

Brethren frowns, still unaware that Faith has flung mug against him at the back. 'Of course not,' he tells the people. 'The Word permits a man to marry a woman and vise versa.'

'You don't tell us what The Word says,' Believer called Judgemental says, ' because we all know what it says. What we are asking you is that how come you proposed to two women in marriage at the same time.'

Brethren is now beginning to feel the effect of the operations of Rumour and Backbiting. 'Can you, please, tell me the other woman that says I proposed to her in marriage?'

'Sister Faith!' Someone among the people says but he cannot really identify the person.

Brethren is hurt as he notes that some people are turning against him. He says, 'Sister Faith is here, I believe.'

'Yes,' Faith says, standing up among the people.

'Did I really propose to marry you, my sister?'

'Yes, sir,' she replies and sits down again.

Brethren feels as if he is stabbed at the back by the same person that is supposed to defend him.

'If you didn't propose to her,' Brother Judgemental who is held in bondage by Principalities warriors of the Dragon called Envy and Jealousy asks, 'how come the news that you're in courtship with her?'

'She's the one that tell people, not me,' Brethren says, feeling very hurt and embarrassed even though three soldiers of Comforter called Love, Longsuffering and humility stand by his side.

'Why didn't you stop her if it's not true?' Brother Critics asks. Like Brother Judgemental, he is also held bound by the Principalities warriors called Variance and Intolerance, making him to rebuke and weaken other Believers, especially those who are just learning to walk in The Spirit.

Judgemental and Critics always wonder why Brethren is always gaining people's attentions. This make them to always look for ways to openly point out his errors and faults so as to prove to the people that he not greater than any of them.

The warriors that hold the two Believers in bondage are tempting Brethren tell everyone at the meeting what actually happened. He almost falls into the temptation to defend himself but Comforter says to him in The Spirit, 'what do you want to achieve if you try to defend yourself?'

'The people need to know the truth,' Brethren says in The Mind.

'You're not in the position to let them know. The rulers of darkness are at war with you. They want you to fight back. Their target is: if they can't get you, they will get the people. Besides, whatever anyone says against you does not reduce you. It will increase you instead if you hold your peace. Keep hold of yourself and save your strength as a giant warrior of The Redeemer for something far more rewarding.'

'Thanks, Comforter,' Brethren says in whisper.

He looks round at the people and smiles at them. 'I am not in the position to defend myself because I don't have the power. The strengths The Redeemer gives to all Believers are meant to help others find their ways to the Lord. If in anyway, any of the things I have said or done has mislead anyone, I am deeply sorry. Please, forgive me. I never mean to hurt or mislead or deal with anyone in the way that is contrary to The Word. Don't focus on me or captivate on my

106

shortcomings because I'm human just like everybody who can make mistakes. Let's all focus on The Redeemer through The Word instead. That's all that counts, isn't it?'

Of course, everybody is moved because Comforter makes them see Humility, Love and Longsuffering around him. Even his accusers cannot say a word until the meeting is over.

CHAPTER EIGHTEEN

Comforter takes Faith to The Spirit through deep sleep to meet The Redeemer who sits under a tree, waiting for her.

She walks slowly towards The Redeemer who looks sad. He gestures her to sit beside him and smiles.

Faith sits down slowly, also looking sad.

'My daughter,' The Redeemer says. She looks at him quietly as if she is aware of what she has done wrong, 'my valuable servant, Brethren is deeply hurt. Why do you think he is hurt?'

'I stabbed him at the back,' she replies quietly.

He smiles. 'Yes,' he says. 'So many people hurt him like that. So it's not a strange thing to him. What makes him feel more hurt is that he expects you to fight the enemies alongside with him, not against him. He loves you to the extent of protecting you, taking the fault that is not really his. He and Hope are down in The Spirit. They do not know what to do again because they are wounded by someone close them.'

She bursts out into emotional sobs. 'I'm so sorry, Lord.'

'It's okay, my daughter,' he says, putting his arm across her shoulder. 'Actually, you're not here to be accused. I just want to let you know that the host of kingdom of Doom are holding series of meetings because of him. They have been hunting for ways to bring him down because I'm using him to terrorize the warriors of Dragon. They shot down his wife because of him after Dragon got permission from The Father. The Father told me to take Gentle home when she is hit. So I have to her take her home and replace her with Hope. I convey this message to Brethren through Gentle. The rulers of darkness get to know my plan to replace Gentle with Hope. So they decided to manipulate the plan. I told Gentle when she is concerned about you that I will also give you a giant as a husband. In fact, he will soon come to you. Before the giant shows, however, you must get out of the mud, which you allowed Principalities warriors of Dragon to get you into.'

Faith cuddles The Redeemer tightly and weeps over his shoulder. 'I will, my Father and my Lord.'

He pats her on the back and continues in a gentle voice, 'there are more to what you see happening in the kingdom of man than what is actually taking place in Eternity kingdom and Dragon's kingdom of Doom. If you walk in The Spirit, you will see so many things that can frighten to the point of asking me to take you home. There is no way you can see much in other kingdoms unless you grow into a matured Believer. The more you grow, the more you will see. The more you see, the more you will see the need to fight Dragon and his warriors. And the more you fight in The Spirit, the more strengths you gather in The Flesh and The Mind. The more strengths you get, the closer you are to the status of a matured Believer or a giant. When you are in any of these levels, you have to keep fighting the enemies until you come home otherwise you'll be brought down.

'The status of my servant, Brethren as a giant warrior is a ver delicate position because the host of Doom kingdom focuses on him. He cannot afford to make mistakes otherwise a lot of people will damn the consequences. He knows that the less he fights, the more chances he gives to the enemies to bring him down. When a giant like him stops fighting the enemies, he becomes weaker. There is a limit of weakness a giant can reach before he starts dying. Before he gets to that limit, I would be forced to take him home. Dragon understands this principle very well. So he wants to get Brethren to that level of weakness and force me to take him home. I don't want to do that yet because I still need him and few other giants I have as warriors.

'When a giant is getting weak, it is a sure sign that he is about to leave the kingdom of man. Dragon is desperately seeking for ways to weaken him since he finds it hard to bring him down. You have to strengthen him because what giants always need are people that would encourage him.

'I have many soldiers, including the giants, the matured and the youth Believers who are all given various assignments, according to their abilities.' He looks at her face, smiling. 'You've been trained to be my soldier. Don't allow the issue of marriage to reduce you into a babe that needs to be fed with milk. You're to fight the enemies of the people with the whole armour of war. You're also going to strengthen other soldiers instead of hurting them.' He smiles again when she nods vigorously. 'You'll go to my servant Brethren and comfort him. Tell him how sorry you are. Then you'll bring him back to his feet. Right now, he is wounded in The Spirit. He needs new strengths. I want to use you to renew his strength.'

Faith shakes with deep emotion as she weeps. 'I feel so terrible about myself and so unworthy of you, Lord.'

'You're special just like everyone that believes in me,' he tells her. 'You're fearfully and wonderfully made. The enemies of mankind are the ones trying to make use of you against others. Just do what I tell you and follow The Word, you'll understand that you're a wonderful person and I love you dearly.'

'I love you too, Lord. Thank you so much for talking to me after all I have done wrong.'

When Faith returns to the kingdom of man, she begins to cry afresh, singing and sobbing emotionally:

I am grateful, oh Lord
For all you have done for me
I am grateful, oh Lord.

I am sorry, oh Lord
I am sorry, oh Lord
Oh, my Redeemer
I am sorry, oh Lord
For all I have done to you
My Redeemer
I am sorry, oh Lord...

She goes to see Brethren at home in the evening. Fortunately, she finds Hope there. Both of them are talking to The Redeemer in The Spirit. She waits for them to finish before she enters the house.

Soon after the courting couple have greeted her, Hope who regards her as someone she needs to avoid makes attempt to take her leave.

'I've come to see two of you, beloved sister,' Faith says gently, feeling sorry that she has become repulsive to the people that love her.

'I'm sorry I have to go now,' Hope says quietly, going towards the door.

Faith goes to block her way. She falls on her kneels. 'Please... It is important to me that we talk. I know I have wronged you. Please find it in your heart to forgive me.'

Hope is so emotionally uplifted that tears of joy and love blind her

110

eyes. She can perceive it at once that she must have met The Redeemer again. Of course, this is what she and Brethren had been praying for since the Lord does not desire the death of anyone but the for everyone to know the truth that will set them free from bondage.

Fath mistakes the tears as the feelings of pains and sorrows. She bursts into hysterical sobs, saying, 'I'm so sorry for hurting you so much....'

Hope pulls her up on her feet and hugs her. 'We've been praying for you... And I can see that The Redeemer has spoken to you. My tears are tears of joy....'

Faith stops crying and asks quietly, 'how do you know the Lord has spoken to me?'

'It's easy to know when someone had been talking to him,' Hope says.

Faith smiles and says, 'you're a great woman. You're going to be as great as mother Gentle whose place you are taking in the life of my giant father over there.' She waves at Brethren who is sitting silently on the couch, looking at them. 'You're greater than I thought. And you're far stronger than me.'

Hope frowns. 'Why are you saying this?'

'You just confirmed that I met with the Lord.'

'And he told you all these?'

'I know through the message he told me to deliver to the two of you. He spoke to me in The Spirit when Comforter took me there through deep sleep.'

'Let's hear it,' Brethren says.

Hope sits close to Brethren while Faith sits opposite them as she narrates all The Redeemer says in The Spirit. In conclusion of the message, she says, 'I would have condemned myself if not for what the Lord says about the rulers of darkness who is trying to make me terrible but I cannot help feeling worthless for trying to bring you down.' She bursts into another round of sobs. 'Despite all the Lord have done to train me through you and The Word, I was still blind of what is happening in The Spirit. Dragon lured me from The Spirit through The Mind into The Flesh and then begin to use me against people that love so much.' She looks at Brethren. 'I remember how I tried to tempt you to...'

'Sister Faith,' Brethren quickly interrupts her, 'you didn't do that, remember?'

Faith look puzzled. 'Are you trying to cover up for me?'

'No,' he replies. 'The Lord has wiped that away with his precious

111

blood. You have no right to refer to that just as no one has the right to bring up any issue that is not in the record of The Father. Anyone that brings it up is definitely working for Dragon who is the accuser of all Believers.'

'I thought all along you are going to use it against me.'

'What?' He looks stunned. 'How can you imagine a thing like that? I don't even remember it.'

'Y- you're - so amazing…' Faith is short of words.

'It's not me sister,' Brethren says. 'It's the amazing grace of The Redeemer that saves a wretch like you and me.'

Hope begins to sing and the rest join her.

> Amazing grace
> How sweet the sound
> That saves a wretch like me…

A few months later Brethren and Hope get married. Of course, Faith is her bridesmaid. Faith's role in the marriage proves to everyone that it is Dragon that is trying to cause problem. Even then, typical of the enemies of mankind, they are always trying to make everything about Believers to work against them.

Few months after the marriage, Faith attends Believer's convention in another town where she meets Faithful, the matured Believer that leads her to The Redeemer some years ago. Faithful has fully grown into a giant that is making exploit for The Redeemer. They had a long chat, sharing many things together through out the days of the convention. Before they leave the convention ground, Comforter had confirmed it to the two of them that The Redeemer plans to make them husband and wife. That year, the marriage takes place and the couple are added to the soldiers that on the assignments to reach out to everybody with the good news of The Redeemer.

CHAPTER NINETEEN

Dragon sits down with the rulers of darkness, looking somewhat frustrated though his council members do not understand why he has to make fuss over minor failures which are inevitable. By now, everyone in all the three kingdoms knows that the kingdom of man had been subdued into playing ground where all kinds of warriors in the levels of Principalities and Powers can have fun. There are replications of Believers' assemblies which serve Dragon or rulers of darkness directly or indirectly. They have their servants who pose as servants of The Redeemer. The lifestyles of most people in the land are nothing but abominations to The Father in Eternity kingdom.

Dragon and his warriors are effectively using countless tools of deceptions and means of destructions like the entertainment, internet and educational institutions to lead people on the path of Doom kingdom. This makes it easy for Principalities warriors to operate in the lives of the people without being conscious of them. The battle is at stage where slaves enjoy the life of bondage and most Believers no longer border about possessing the mansions and the rewards The Redeemer promises them in Eternity kingdom. No matured Believer needs to be informed that the kingdom of man is on the verge of total and eternal destruction. By now, Dragon is having countless number of warriors, including mortal servants that are working for him, fighting The Redeemer who have come to deliver them. The number of Believers that are actually terrorizing Dragon and his warriors continues to drop everyday. The effect of that is to have much people ending up in Doom kingdom when they depart the kingdom of man. In fact, going by the record that is revealed to some Believers in The Spirit where they can easily perceive what is happening in all the kingdoms, the number of people going to Doom kingdom and Eternity kingdom is ratio 1000 to 1.

Various areas of kingdom of man is now filled with mortals since

113

its inception, which suppose to earn The Redeemer more soldiers that will combat the enemies but it only add more to the mortal warriors of the Dragon.

Dragon and the rulers of darkness have so designed their weapons of mass destructions that they hardly fail to wreck havoc in all areas of life of mankind. They go as far as enlisting children, youths and even old people in the battle against The Father who gives them life. Through so many sophisticated means like secularism that makes the battles in The Flesh, The Mind and The Spirit appears like mere religion, most people are blindfolded. Even when they feel the effect of the battles in The Flesh and The Mind, they readily accept anything, however stupid or irrational, as explanations of all events. In fact, a lot of Believers are so deceived that they are now skeptical about The Redeemer coming to take them to Eternity kingdom as he promises them in The Word. They feel so comfortable in The Flesh and in The Mind that they forget about most of the things in The Spirit and in The Word. Much more others are already unconscious to the point of death, if not completely dead in The Spirit. Some of these spiritually unconscious or dead people are decamping to the side of Dragon without having the slightest idea of what they are doing. This invariably gives enemies of real Believers upper hand, making the war against them seems like the battle of Armagedon.

Despite wrecking so much havoc on mankind, Dragon is still determined to cause much more eternal catastrophe. If possible, he wants every mortal to end up in Doom kingdom. So he works tirelessly to keep every of them busy, marking the people for himself with the ingenious mark of the beast through technologies.

According to the prophecy in The Word, all genuine Believers would need to be taken away by The Redeemer before he is given the chance to mark the people for eternal destruction with the real mark of the beast. He knows he cannot alter anything in The Word. He also knows that he does not need to go to the courtroom in Eternity to get permission before he gives the ingenious mark to people. He can hide under what The Redeemer says in The Word in Matthew Chapter 24 verses 5 to 31. He says in the passages, "For many shall come in my name, saying, I am The Redeemer; and shall deceive many.

" And ye shall hear of wars and rumours of wars: see that ye be not troubled: for all these things must come to pass, but the end is not yet.

"For nation shall rise against nation, and kingdom against kingdom: and there shall be famines, and pestilences, and

114

earthquakes, in divers places.

"All these are the beginning of sorrows.

"Then shall they deliver you up to be afflicted, and shall kill you: and ye shall be hated of all nations for my name's sake.

"And then shall many be offended, and shall betray one another, and shall hate one another.

"And many false Believers shall rise, and shall deceive many.

"And because iniquity shall abound, the love of many shall wax cold.

"But he that endure unto the end, the same shall be saved.

"And The Word shall be preached in all the kingdom of man for a witness unto all nations; and then shall the end come.

"When ye therefore shall see the abomination of desolation, spoken of by Daniel the Believer, stand in the holy place, (whoso readeth, let him understand:)

"Then let them which be in Judaea flee into the mountains:

"Let him which is on the housetop not come down to take any thing out of his house:

"Neither let him which is in the field return back to take his clothes.

"And woe unto them that are with child, and to them that give suck in those days!

"But pray ye that your flight be not in the winter, neither on the sabbath day:

"For then shall be great tribulation, such as was not since the beginning of the kingdom of man to this time, no, nor ever shall be.

"And except those days should be shortened, there should no flesh be saved: but for the elect's sake those days shall be shortened.

"Then if any man shall say unto you, Lo, here is The Redeemer, or there; believe it not.

"For there shall arise false Redeemers, and false Believers, and shall show great signs and wonders; insomuch that, if it were possible, they shall deceive the very elect.

"Behold, I have told you before.

"Wherefore if they shall say unto you, Behold, he is in the desert; go not forth: behold, he is in the secret chambers; believe it not.

"For as the lightning cometh out of the east, and shineth even unto the west; so shall also my coming.

"For wheresoever the carcase is, there will the eagles be gathered together.

"Immediately after the tribulation of those days shall the sun be

115

darkened, and the moon shall not give her light, and the stars shall fall from heaven, and the powers of Eternity shall be shaken:

"And then shall appear the sign of me from Eternity kingdom: and then shall all the tribes of the earth mourn, and they shall see me coming in the clouds of Eternity with power and great glory.

"And I shall send my angels with a great sound of a trumpet, and they shall gather together my elect from the four winds, from one end of kingdom to the other."

The words of The Redeemer are the basis of operations of Dragon and the rulers of darkness so far. If he can get a way to hypnotize the mortals, including Believers with the ingenious marks that are similar in characteristics to the mark of the beast that is recorded in The Word in Revelation chapter thirteen verses sixteen and seventeen, the trick to deceive and eventually destroy will apply. The Word in the passage says, "And he (the beast) causes all, both small and great, rich and poor, free and bond, to receive a mark in their right hand, or in their foreheads: And that no man might buy or sell, save he that had the mark, or the name of the beast, or the number of his name. "

Dragon looks excited as he muses over the passage. Though he is obliged to follow the truth that is revealed to mankind in The Word, he is still anxious to mark the people for himself. He would have to come up with the ingenious marks through various forms of inventions, ideas and technologies that will blindfold the people until The Redeemer comes to take Believers to Eternity.

With the prophecies in The Word, Dragon knows that he does not need to obtain permission from The Father before he gives the people the ingenious marks.

'We're going to introduce ingenious marks of the beast to the people,' he tells the rulers of darkness.

Ignorance looks confused. 'What's ingenious mark, my lord?'

Dragon explains it to them as he plans it.

'It's so complicated that I'm confused,' Ignorance says.

'You're not supposed to get confused, you fool. You're to confuse the mortals,' Dragon says. 'An ingenious mark is something similar to the mark of the beast in The Word.'

Compromise is thoughtful as he asks, 'my lord, are we supposed to do that now or after The Redeemer has taken all Believers away?'

'We are not supposed to give them the real mark now,' Dragon replies. 'We just want to confuse and convince everybody, including Believers that either The Redeemer has come or no longer coming.

116

As he delays in coming, we have the opportunities to distort the truths in The Word, manipulate the prophesies and deceive the people with our own versions of everything about Eternity kingdom. We will give them ingenious marks of the beast through technologies that will hypnotize them. With the use of technologies, we will keep the mortals busy till The Redeemer comes. When he comes, he will hardly find anyone ready to go with him. Once the people are not ready, it would be too late for everyone that is kept busy to follow him.'

'Are the ingenious marks meant for destruction?' Ignorance asks.

'No,' Dragon sounds irritated by the question. 'The real mark of destruction is to be given to the people by the beast, which we are preparing for a release after The Redeemer has taken all Believers away from the kingdom of man. The ingenious marks I'm talking about have similar characteristics with the mark of the beast. They will be given to the mortals through flashy beasts in the form of technologies. The marks are to keep them busy and hypnotized, making them to forget about Eternity kingdom.'

'What if a giant like Brethren exposes the plan or raise people that would counter this plan, using the same technologies?' Disobedience asks.

'You always overrate the strengths of giant Believers because they often get victories but you fail to see them as mortals who also enjoy things in the kingdom of man. Anyway, I want you to see the situation this way: the people, especially our slaves are made to see things of The Redeemer and The Word as mere religion instead of seeing him as their Saviour and The Word as the way of living. Ignorance with his warriors are going to hide vital truths from the people, including Believers who are expected to know better. For this reasons, slaves and Believers will be yoked together on the social media on the internet, social clubs, entertainments, means of communication and education where they will be hypnotized and brainwashed with the same materials all in the name of knowledge, amusements, information and interactions.'

He smiles when they look excited. 'You know, these mortals are so blind that they can't even imagine we exist in anyway. Anyone that tries to prove our existence through what they can perceive as our operations is considered paranoid or insane. This blindness is what we are going to use as our major weapon to lead them to Doom kingdom, where we'll torture them for all eternity!'

'Yeeh!' The rulers cheer him.

He raises up his hand and continues, 'Ignorance has a very important assignment here. The Word of The Redeemer mandate all Believers to study and use it as a sword to fight us. When they are disarmed of The Word, they will be moved from offensive into defensive position where we can easily strike them.'

He looks at Heresy. 'Heresy, you're to twist the truth in The Word if at all Ignorance cannot get it from them. Through that, most people will be blindfolded. They will never recognize the truth even when they see it. They will not understand prophecy of The Word coming to fulfillment. With this lack of understanding or knowledge of the truth, the mortals, including most Believers will end up in Doom kingdom before they know it.'

He looks at the rest of the rulers of darkness. 'All of you must find more ways to enthrone our mortal servants as kings in all parts of kingdom of man. We can easily use them to enslave the people through legislation and policies that work against The Redeemer and Believers. They will persecute Believers and make them suffer if they will do not obey the law that makes them go against The Word.

'I understand recently that most of you have paid too much attention to individual mortals. This time, we want to destroy them in mass with our ingenious marks. We'll encroach and crush them in mass. There should be more bloodshed in The Flesh, more casualties in The Mind and more deaths in The Spirit. In this end-time, we will cause much more crisis, much more conflicts, much more sufferings and much more pains in all parts of the kingdom of man. When the suffering is much, even Believers will come to us for solution. Compromise will ensure that all Believers who cannot endure to the end will end up in Doom kingdom. As for those who have the stamina to endure to the end, we will increase their sufferings and use others to persecuted them at every side. By the time The Redeemer comes back, he will hardly find anyone called Believers again.'

After the presentations, the rulers of darkness burst into uproar for the brilliant idea, praising Dragon.

CHAPTER TWENTY

There is a Believers' conference, organized by high level and seasoned warriors of The Redeemer. The speakers, which include giants like Brethren, Faithful, Sanctified and matured Believers like Hope, Faith, Justified, Beloved and a host of others who are well grounded in The Word and seasoned in secular affairs at the same time. Their presentations which will be broadcasted through out the kingdom of man are specially packaged with the sole objectives of educating and warning mankind of the battle in The Flesh, The Mind and The Spirit. Because some of the speakers are medical doctor, lawyer and professionals in other secular affairs, they have more than enough materials to prove of the existence of the unseen enemies of mankind.

Doom kingdom just like Eternity kingdom is known by different names like Hell, Hades, Sheol, Lake Of Fire and A Place Of Agony. Eternity kingdom is also known as Heaven, Kingdom Of God and Heavenly Places. The kingdom of man is also known as The World and The Earth. The Father is also known by many names like Almighty God, God The Father, Jehovah and a host of others. The Redeemer is also known by names like Jesus Christ, The Son Of God, God The Son, Lord of lords, King of kings, Emmanuel, Wonderful, Counselor, Prince Of Peace and others. Comforter is also known as Holy Spirit, Spirit Of God, God The Spirit, Holy Ghost and others like that. Dragon is known as Lucifer, Satan, Devil, Old Serpent and many others. Dragon's numerous warriors are also known by many names like Demons, Devils, Evil Spirits, Fallen Angels, Unclean Spirits, Spirits Of Bondage and others.

The conference is one of the most important meetings in the gatherings of all Believers in the modern days because it is aimed at putting into light what is happening in The Spirit, possibly using The Word to restore so many things that had been distorted or destroyed

119

by Dragon. The meeting is also aimed at charging warriors of The Redeemer that would launch counter attack against the vast armies of Dragon, which include the mortals and the immortals.

The battles all Believers have to face now are getting more and more fierce by the day with millions of soldiers of The Redeemer either falling or heading to Doom kingdom. The latest of the onslaught against mankind is the introduction of the ingenious marks of the beast. By now many Believers are desperately looking out for the return of The Redeemer or the Angels to come and take them away to the mansions that are prepared for them in Eternity kingdom.

Each of the speakers shares The Word, equips Believers and assures them of the mercy of The Father who is aware that all mortals are nothing but dust.

Brethren is the first speaker. He greets every participant and thanks them briefly before he begins to present his paper. 'The purpose of this conference is not to raise false alarm but to draw our attentions to some crucial things that are happening all over the world.

'With reference to what is happening around us, I would like to read the book of Revelation chapter twelve verse twelve which says, "Therefore rejoice, ye heavens, and ye that dwell in them. Woe to the inhabiters of the earth and of the sea! for the devil is come down unto you, having great wrath, because he knoweth that he hath but a short time."'

Brethren looks round at Believers. There are so many of them in attendance. Most of them appear confused about the trend of things. It seems the tide in the battle is turning against all Believers and very few seem to understand what is happening. They come to the conference with the hope that they will get answers to so many difficult questions and be refreshed and be more equipped for battles against their unseen enemies. These who are conscious of the fact that they are soldiers of The Redeemer know that a lot of people are counting on them to lead them to Eternity kingdom. Hence, getting answers to so many troubling questions will help them find their bearings and footings in the battle.

'Fellow soldiers of The Redeemer,' Brethren says, 'with exception of none, we are all guilty of many things. We're not up and doing in things of Eternity kingdom. A lot of us have been fighting mortals we are supposed to help as if they are our enemies. We have failed to realize that no mortal is an enemy of mortal. Our immortal enemies are the ones that turn us against one another. They make us ignorance of the fact that we are actually fighting The Redeemer if we

120

fight one another. Because he loves us, he comes to deliver all mortals. He is unwilling to lose anyone. Instead he wants everyone to know the truth that will liberate us from the enemies of mankind.

'Most of us who have been fighting in The Flesh have actually been blindfolded and used against one another, even though we all think we are trying to please the Lord. The Word tells us in Hosea chapter four verse six that the people of the Lord perish for lack of knowledge. The enemies of mortals have designed sophisticated means of making us much more conscious of our kingdom than the kingdom of Eternity. These things can penetrate into our minds through the use of the gateways called Eyes, Ears, Noses, Mouths and Flesh. Because we easily perceive these things through these gateways to our minds, vast majority of mortals are not conscious of things in The Spirit. Even then The Word warns us in First John chapter two verse fifteen, "Love not the world, neither the things that are in the world. If any man love the world, the love of The Father is not in him." ' He pauses for a while, pacing round on the platform and looking thoughtful.

The people are completely silent, paying keen attention to every word as if their victories in the battle depends on it.

'The gateways into our minds are the major problems of all mortals, including you and me. They make us more vulnerable to the weapons of mass destructions and make us more conscious of ourselves. Through these gateways, we can be deceived and manipulated. Unless all Believers learn to keep these gateways safe against the enemies, we will fall victims just like the rest of the mortals. These gateways are easy way to err and make us selfish without even knowing it. We've all made mistakes of allowing these gateways to get the better part of us.' Brethren again pauses briefly before he continues. 'I want to confess my mistake to you as a mortal, which probably will make us understand how much we need Comforter and the whole armour of war before we can continue to get victories for ourselves and for others.

'When The Redeemer took my wife to Eternity kingdom, I felt so bad that I told the Lord, he either returns my wife to me or he takes me home. I actually didn't want him to return her. I wanted him to take me home because I was sick and tired of what is happening in the world.

'I waited for him in the hospital room where my dead wife laid. What I got as a reply is not what I bargained for. The Redeemer sent back my wife with an angel that accompanied her.' Brethren is unexpectedly overcome with emotion. With tears stained eyes, he

121

says, 'my wife brought a message from The Redeemer. It is a message of hope, love and joy in Eternity kingdom. He said he would have loved to take me home but my assignment is yet to be completed. If he had taken me home, chances are that you will not hear what I'm telling you now.

'It is natural to be selfish and look for an escape route when there is much pains to be endured, much deaths of mortals to witness and much sorrows to go through in the kingdom of man. As mortals, we will naturally want to escape from these catastrophe, especially if we are very conscious that we are on our way to Eternity kingdom where eternal bliss and joy await us. The inability to answer this question makes us guilty: "what about the rest of the mortals?" Many of us who know the differences between Eternal kingdom and kingdom of man will naturally want to go home. If we think of our home - the mansions that are prepared for us in Eternity kingdom, how about the rest of the mortals that are going to Doom? What are we doing to help them escape to Eternity kingdom? We must understand this: the battle is not about The Redeemer! His love for the mortals brings him in. It is not about Eternity kingdom because it is a place of eternal peace and joy. It is not about the kingdom of man because it is going to be destroyed sooner or later! It is not about us because we have been redeemed and assured of our inheritance in Eternity kingdom! It is not about Dragon because he knows he had been condemned to Doom. But it is about mortals that are caught in crossfire, going on the journey to Doom kingdom!

'We were all once heading to the place of Doom kingdom until The Redeemer leaves his glory and honour in Eternity kingdom to deliver us from the enemies that are by far stronger than us. He takes time to build and equip us into warriors because he wants to count on us to reach out to other mortals and deliver them so that they will also be partakers of Eternity kingdom. Out of sheer selfishness, everybody including me begins to nurse his or her wounds instead of fighting to save as The Word teaches. We leave other mortals at the mercy of our enemies, which we all know hate everyone of us with passion. We forget easily what the Lord has done for us on the cross of calvary. We forget the fact that this war will determine the eternal destinations of other mortals.

'The Redeemer can only use Believers against our immortal enemies. Because the Lord knows our weakness as mortals, he gives us Comforter that will help us fight like the immortal warriors who put on the invisible amour of war. Comforter always want to take us to The

Spirit where we can easily get victories but we always want to stay in The Comfort Zone, which is located in The Flesh. Anyone staying or walking or fighting in The Flesh is fighting on the wrong side. He cannot see himself in danger, let alone to see other mortals dying everyday.

'The gateways to our mind, which we have failed to keep safe bring about our selfishness and quest for comfort; thereby making us to sacrifice other mortals which actually bring The Redeemer into the battle. All these in addition with other things makes us all guilty of many things.

'Having shared with you the background of all the presentations in this conference, I would now refer to the passage I read to you in the book of Revelation chapter twelve verse twelve where we are made to understand that the enemy has come down to us with great anger because he knows he has short time. He has a short time to subdue and take mortals to Doom kingdom. Our secular environment may not see things in our way but we all know that the kingdom of man is under serious attack in all areas. We have read about perilous times in second Timothy chapter three verse one as signs of the beginning of the end but how many Believers are really conscious of this as we experience these events? Believers have had issues with one another, ranging from denominational differences to interpretations of The Word. I know that there are different schools of thoughts with regards to so many things about Eternity kingdom, Doom kingdom and kingdom of man. We must not dwell on our differences but dwell rather on the common ground of all Believers which is The Word. Even though a lot of people that are serving Dragon without knowing it are seriously perverting The Word. The Redeemer says in John chapter ten verse fourteen, "I know my sheep and my sheep know me." I want you to listen to the voice of the Lord in this conference rather than the voice of men or that of Dragon outside the fold of The Redeemer.

'A lot of things which had been foretold by The Word about two thousand years ago are coming to past in our generation. Since we have been informed beforehand, we need not to be surprised nor fight against the prophesy but rather to know what we are supposed to do.

'Believers need to be like children of Issachar in First Chronicles chapter twelve verse thirty-two in The Word. The passage says, "And of the children of Issachar, which were men that had understanding of the times, to know what Israel ought to do; the heads of them were two hundred; and all their brethren were at their commandment."

'I want you to, please, note three things in this lecture, which are

123

these:

'Firstly, we must note that the kingdom of man is no longer our home. We are sojourners who are just passing through it. All mortals are heading either towards Eternal Kingdom or Doom kingdom. The way to Eternity kingdom as we all know is narrow. The Redeemer tells us in The Word in Matthew chapter seven verses thirteen and fourteen that narrow is the way that leads to Eternity kingdom while the way to Doom is wide and broad. Very few people, according to The Word take the narrow way. The reality of this passage is that most mortals will end up in Doom kingdom. This is very hard to believe, considering all the Lord has done to save all morals. Of course, The Redeemer gives us the power and the opportunity to reduce those heading to Doom but I must confess to you that it is never going to be that easy. The reason is that all mortals, with exception of none are blind. What actually gives Believers sights and insights is Comforter who reveals all things to us. Anyone without Comforter will not be different from other mortals. Because the mortals we are trying to reach are blind even though most of them believe they can see, we will have problems in making them see what we can see with the sight of Comforter. We do not have to blame them in any way because The Word tells us in Second Corinthians chapter four verse four to expect them to be so blind. The passage says, "in whom the god of this world hath blinded the minds of them which believe not, lest the light of the glorious gospel of Christ, who is the image of God, should shine unto them."

'The lack of knowledge of the truth about Eternity kingdom will make mortals like us call us names, hate us and even attack us. Why is this so? The answer leads us to the next thing we must note.

'The second thing to note in this lecture is that the kingdom of man have turned into battlefields. There is fierce war between Eternity kingdom and Eternal Doom over all mortals. The bad news is that the mortal warriors that are serving the purpose of our immortal enemies have by far outnumbered the real armies of The Redeemer. In fact, with way things are going, if all Believers are not made to understand what is going on in The Spirit, we will soon find ourselves fighting one another with the same weapons, which we are supposed to use to rescue other mortals.

'Our immortal enemies have all kinds of powers to oppress every Believer, ranging from political to economic powers. Dragon ensures that his mortal warriors are at the helms of affairs in all areas of kingdom of man. He uses the immortals to attack all Believers at all

124

levels. He has no respect for your status. So let us not make issues out of that and be focused on dealing with him with our amour of war, giving room for Comforter to direct us since he is the one that sees what we cannot see.

'Under this point, I want you to note that our immortal enemies have turned lots of warriors of The Redeemer into entertainers who are supposed to see the battles in The Spirit, The Mind and The Flesh as very serious issues. A lot of them abandon The Word that can be used to librate other mortals and appeal to the emotions and intellects of mortals. They are so blindfolded that they do not realize that mortals will damn the eternal consequences of their actions. Their massages often times cause complications in the lives of their audiences, making the real message of The Redeemer unacceptable to them.

'The Word says in Second Timothy chapter three verses one to seven, "This know also, that in the last days perilous times shall come.

"For men shall be lovers of their own selves, covetous, boasters, proud, blasphemers, disobedient to parents, unthankful, unholy,

"Without natural affection, trucebreakers, false accusers, incontinent, fierce, despisers of those that are good,

"Traitors, heady, highminded, lovers of pleasures more than lovers of God;

"Having a form of godliness, but denying the power thereof: from such turn away.

"For of this sort are they which creep into houses, and lead captive silly women laden with sins, led away with divers lusts,

"Ever learning, and never able to come to the knowledge of the truth."

'There are few things we must note in this passage which has to do with Principalities warriors of Dragon. While these warriors are bringing down or misleading so many Believers in the class of babes and youths, matured Believers and giants must be particularly careful and watchful of warriors like Ignorance, Disunity, Vanities, Arrogance, Indiscipline, Compromise, Selfishness, Self-Glory, Prayerlessness and a host of others. However strong we are, any of these warriors of Dragon can get us down if we allow them to engage us in the battle. We must fight Ignorance with The Word which is the sword of The Spirit, fight Arrogance with Humility and fight Vanities by Righteousness, which is part of our amour of war. We must fight Disunity with Love and Tolerance.

'Love, as you all know is the most powerful and greatest of all gifts The Father gives us. It is Love that brings The Redeemer down from Eternity to redeem all mortals from Dragon, making us worthy to enter Eternity kingdom when we leave this world. We must, therefore, love the Lord, love one another and love all mortals, no matter who they are. The Redeemer says in John chapter thirteen verses thirty-four to thirty five, "A new commandment I give unto you, That you love one another; as I have loved you, that ye also love one another.

"By this shall all men know that ye are my disciples, if you have love one to another."

'The Lord makes us to understand that Love is powerful. For this reason, he commands us to love one another. Without Love, we can never go extra mile to reach out to other mortals with the truth that will set them free. Without Love, we can never have access to the power of The Redeemer which we need before we can defeat Dragon and his warriors. Without Love, we can never come together as one and launch an attack against these immortal enemies that are determine destroy us. They give us reason to hate one another because they wants to weaken Love that gives us strength. The language of Love is simple enough for everyone to comprehend, including the mortals that are turned against us but very few people even among Believers can communicate it. All Believers need to learn how to communicate Love to others if we want to be effective in our walk with the Lord and in our quest to reach out to other mortals.

'The final thing I want you to note in this lecture is that the beast is already out to label mortals with marks that are similar to the mark of the beast, going by what The Redeemer reveals to me. Through these marks, Dragon hopes to put all mortals in a state of stupor, using his numerous warriors that are both visible and invisible to reign over everybody.' He pauses to look round at the people. Many of them wear puzzled expressions.

'What we see in the world today are actually marks that will keep mortals occupied in Vanities and things that have no eternal values. These things, as good as they seem are marks of Dragon with the sole aim of destroying as many mortals as are deceived.

'All Believers, especially the matured ones and giants are faced with issues of proving all these claims, despite the evidences around us. These issues make us to understand that while some Believers are busy fighting one another or doing other things, Dragon and his warriors are busy brainwashing, deceiving and manipulating the mortals. Thus we are seeing the fulfilment of the passage in Second Timothy chapter three verse twelve, which says, "Yea, and all that will live godly in Christ Jesus shall suffer persecution. But evil men and

126

seducers shall wax worse and worse, deceiving, and being deceived."

'Because we have failed to reach out to these mortals that are deceived, according to the passage, they are deceived to the point of serving Dragon's purpose of deceptions.

'In spite of all these, there is hope for all mortals, including you and me which is found in The Word in Mark chapter sixteen verse fifteen to eighteen. The Lord says in the passage, "Go ye into all the world, and preach The Word to every mortal.

"He that believeth and is baptized shall be saved; but he that believeth not shall be damned.

"And these signs shall follow them that believe; In my name shall they cast out devils; they shall speak with new tongues;

"They shall take up serpents; and if they drink any deadly thing, it shall not hurt them; they shall lay hands on the sick, and they shall recover."

'All Believers had been given the power to save and deliver other mortals. The hope in the world lies with all Believers. If we use this power as instructed by The Redeemer, all mortals stand the chance of getting deliverance from Dragon and his warriors that are holding them bond. If we don't use it, however, they do not stand any chance of survival. If they die in the battlefield and end up in Doom kingdom, The Word already spells the consequence for us in Ezekiel chapter three verses eighteen to twenty-one. The passage says, "When I say unto the wicked, Thou shalt surely die; and thou givest him not warning, nor speakest to warn the wicked from his wicked way, to save his life; the same wicked man shall die in his iniquity; but his blood will I require at thine hand.

"Yet if thou warn the wicked, and he turn not from his wickedness, nor from his wicked way, he shall die in his iniquity; but thou hast delivered thy soul.

"Again, When a righteous man doth turn from his righteousness, and commit iniquity, and I lay a stumbling-block before him, he shall die: because thou hast not given him warning, he shall die in his sin, and his righteousness which he hath done shall not be remembered; but his blood will I require at thine hand.

"Nevertheless if thou warn the righteous man, that the righteous sin not, and he doth not sin, he shall surely live, because he is warned; also thou hast delivered thy soul."

'We can see it from this passage that if we do not preach to the rest of the mortals and deliver them from eternal death in Doom, our hands will be filled with their blood.

127

'We have heard and read The Word. We has no reason, therefore to be indifferent of what is happening in the world.

'I would like to round up this lecture with what I experienced some years ago. I was completely down in The Spirit. I don't want to die there. So I requested the Lord to take me home. To make me understand the implication of what I requested from him, he took me home out The Flesh. I found myself facing the gate of Eternity kingdom but before I was allowed to enter, a large number of what look like mortals blocked my way. They all said I have no right whatsoever to enter the glorious city of Eternity kingdom while they are left to languish in Doom kingdom. I wondered what business I have to do with them until the Lord explained to me that they are mortals I am supposed to reach with The Word while in the world. Unless I reach out to them, they will end up in Doom kingdom and I would be required to account for their lives. Since that time, I realize that if we don't reach out to other mortals, we can be denied access to Eternity kingdom.' He pauses for a long time as the audience ponder over all they hear. Then he says in conclusion, 'our major offence against our Lord and Saviour is our refusal to reach out to other mortals. We make not know that we have offended The Redeemer but we know now. Since we now know, let us go to him and ask for his forgiveness while the next speaker gets prepared to deliver his paper.'

All Believers in attendance stand on their feet as they begin to talk to The Redeemer, asking for his forgiveness.

128

CHAPTER TWENTY-ONE

While Believers are still holding meeting, Dragon and his council members are having serious deliberations on how to launch more attacks against Believers.

Dragon looks thoughtful as he brood over all his plans. His schemes appear so complicated and sophisticated that no one else except him understands them. Going by what The Redeemer says in The Word, there will be two different tribulation periods. The first period is before all Believers are taken away to Eternity kingdom. The second period would be after they are gone. When they are gone, the beast which will give mortals the real mark would be released. The best time to reduce the number of mortals heading to Eternity kingdom is during the first period. During the second period, he would have full control over everything about mortals, ranging from political to economic setup.

He does not have the full control over all the mortals during the first tribulation because of the presence of Believers who have the powers to contend with him and his warriors. He knows that all Believers that follow The Word can easily defeat him in any of the battlefields. This is the main reason Believers that adhere to The Word are major threats. Thus he would need to make the first tribulation period a battle of wits. He would empower all his mortal warriors with wealth, wisdom and skills to invent so many glamourous looking visuals that will condition mortals to accept lies as truths, unholy as holy and magical as wonderful things. He would have to lure all the mortals through what they can perceive with their human senses. He would make Believers reconsider their stand against him by making them see what they are losing if remain Believers.

'We are not going to leave any stone unturned,' Dragon tells the rulers of darkness. 'The warriors of The Redeemer are having serious talks on how to launch counter attack against us through out the

129

kingdom of man. Comforter is revealing to them a lot of our secret plans, including what we are doing in the first period of tribulation.'

'We are doing all we can to hide the plans, aren't we, my lord?' Ignorance asks.

'Yes, we are,' Dragon says. 'You and your team are doing fine job to hide vital information in The Word from them. Still, there are matured Believers and giants that are determined to reach out to other mortals and rescue them from us. We can't afford to let them continue like that because we have little time at this first period of tribulation to lure Believers from The Redeemers.' He looks at Ignorance. 'I'm counting on you to keep them perpetually ignorant of what The Word says and what they are supposed to do.

Dragon looks thoughtful.

Compromise says, 'I have an idea of how we can tackle them.'

He and the rest of the rulers of darkness look at him with interests.

'Tell us about your idea?' Dragon says at once.

'Well,' Compromise says, 'I think if we shoot darts like poverty, failures, frustrations and others at them in The Flesh and The Mind, I and other warriors like Indiscipline can work on Believers at all levels. If at all we don't make them shift their stand with The Redeemer, we can always make them ineffective in their quest to reach out to other mortals.'

'How?' Dragon is eager to know.

'If Believers are frustrated or made poor or made to fail in their endeavours, some of them can be discouraged. Those who are not discouraged can easily be lured into the system of rat race which we have been using for ages to keep all mortals busy through out their lives.'

'Yes,' Dragon says slowly, looking deeply thoughtful. 'Rat race... Yes. I think I love the idea of getting all Believers involved in the system of rat race. The idea is very good if it can be polished it to suit our purpose.' He pauses, nodding with satisfactions.' He looks round at the rest. 'The idea is bound to work.'

'We are not sure of that, my lord, are we?' Doubt who is recently invited to work with the rulers of darkness says. 'What we know about matured Believers and giants are frightening enough.'

'What do you know about them?' Dragon roars at him. There is silence. He bellows at him, 'tell me!'

'Nothing much, my lord.'

'Let me educate you on one or two things about mortals. They

130

are not a smart as you think you think, you know. Even though they read so much things about us and The Redeemer in The Word, most of them do not understand what they read, let alone to believe it. Teaching and making them to believe is quite a task for Believers. Do you know how they get to their blind condition?'

Doubt says, 'no, my lord.'

'We've been working for centuries to give them false evidence of something that is not real. We've concealed real things with what they can see and convince them that what they cannot see is not real. We always rule them with weapons of Fear and Deceptions while The Redeemer attracts and rules them with Love. While The Redeemer is using Believers to contend with us over other mortals by making them to follow The Word, we have no law to follow in fighting them. We have the power to steal the body of mortals, kill them in The Spirit and destroy them in Doom kingdom. Do you understand that lesson, you moron?'

'Yes, my lord,' Doubt replies quickly.

'I brought you here to work with us, not to ask senseless questions. Your work is to weaken the faith of all Believers. We've introduced ingenious marks into the kingdom of man. You must make best use of it against as many Believers that give you the chance. Use what they can perceive to make them question The Word and doubt if everything they know about The Redeemer is true.' He looks round at the rest before he says, 'as Compromise suggests, we are going to design different sophisticated means of rat race that will engage Believers. While using economy as a rope to pull as many mortals into the race, we'll use ego for some and use selfishness to rope others. If a mortal survive one, he or she cannot survive the others.'

Dragon gives indulgent smiles when he sees most of the rulers of darkness looking impressed. 'I was at the courtroom recently where The Father decides that it is about time he brings the kingdom of man to an end but The Redeemer pleads for more time. He wants to give more people chance to make it to Eternity kingdom but we are turning everything against him. Instead of the mortals, especially the slaves to size the opportunity to go to The Redeemer, we are using things they can see to lure them away from him. Despite all the signs of the end time, the people are still indifferent.' He looks at Apostasy and smiles at him. 'You're doing a good job but you need to keep it up'. He looks round at the rest. 'You're all doing very well but we are yet to strike our deadest blow.'

As Dragon and the rulers of darkness consider the various ways

131

to reduce the number of Believers, the matured ones and the giants continue to educate one another, interpreting the present events in line with The Word.

Hope, Brethren's wife is addressing the audience, trying to explain a few things about one of the ingenious marks of Dragon that is related to medicine. The mark which is introduced into some areas of kingdom of man is called Radio Frequency Identification. With her experience in medical field and in The Word, she attempts to bring into light the prophecy in The Word as it relates to modern technologies.

'Some areas of kingdom of man had been introduced into microchips which are to be planted in the body of mortals,' Hopes says. 'Some of the reasons for doing this include tracking people down if they are kidnapped, guard against Alzheimer's, prevent medical mistakes, making it easy to track down criminals…. The list of its so-called benefits goes on and on. As good as these reasons sounds, the similar characteristics of this microchip with mark of the beast make a lot of mortals assume that it is the real mark of the beast. Thus many mortals, especially Believers kick against the policy of implanting it into their bodies. This is a good move, not because it the real mark of the beast but because the source of the mark is the same as both - from Dragon. Secondly, it is very risky for Believers to accept it or to allow it to be implanted into mortals for a number of reasons.

'The first reason is that this identification chip or Radio Frequency Identification chip known as RFID is designed in such a way that it can go beyond what anyone can imagine. From my research work, RFID can do much more than what people understand it to be. As a scientist and medical practitioner, I believe RFID can go as far as monitoring and even influencing what is going on in the brains of mortals. In other words, if a person is not doing Dragon's bidding, the technology will discover this.

'Secondly, if anyone allows himself to be implanted, he can be controlled like a remote-controlled robot because the chip is sophisticated enough to control what you think or believe.

'A stronger point to note here is that Believers who are implanted with this type of chips would be brainwashed and used to fight along side with Dragon's mortal warriors. Even if they see themselves as Believers, they will constantly contend with The Word.

'I'll like to prove these points with some of my findings while studying the characteristics of this microchip.

'I discovered in my studies that part of RFID makes it unnecessary to carry with you any traditional identification like P.I.N numbers to access your bank account.' She pauses for a while, thinking of the best way to make the presentations simple enough for everyone to understand. 'I'm counting on Comforter to make this paper comprehensible enough. Let me define what biometric in simple terms before we juxtapose it with the point I'm trying to mark.

'Biometric is a means to identify a person through measuring a particular physical or behavioural characteristics which belong to many people. The advantages of biometric system over traditional identification include the fact that a person does not have to present anything except himself before he is identified. Secondly, the critical variables for identification is the most accurate. So there is no possible way of falsification. Figures are always used in addition to other characteristics in this means of identification. Hence RFID carries figures as part of means to identify a person.

'The microchip is capable of doing many things that are yet to be discovered but it has been proven through experiments that it can be uses to control human thoughts and actions. Invariably, the chip can deny the host of his or her power of free choice. If this power is allowed to be taken away from any mortal through implantations of this type of microchips, getting rid of it will take major miracle from the Lord. This is not to say, however, that the case is hopeless. The adage that says in medical cases: Prevention Is Better Than Cure applies to the case of the microchip.

'The possible deliverance of all mortals that are implanted with the microchip is one of the things that make it different from the real mark of the beast. The fate of anyone who takes the real mark after Believers had been taken to Eternity kingdom is spelt out in Revelation chapter sixteen verses one and two. The passage says, "And I heard a great voice out of the temple saying to the seven angels, Go your ways, and pour out the vials of the wrath of God upon the earth.

"And the first went, and poured out his vial upon the earth; and there fell a noisome and grievous sore upon the men which had the mark of the beast, and upon them which worshipped his image."

'In Revelation chapter nineteen verse twenty, The Word says, "And the beast was taken, and with him the false prophet that wrought miracles before him, with which he deceived them that had received the mark of the beast, and them that worshipped his image. These both were cast alive into a lake of fire burning with brimstone."

'Going by these passages, we can conclude that anyone with the real mark of the beast is far from redemption or deliverance. It is

133

possible that a scanty number of people may be able to withstand the pressure of not taking the real mark of the beast during the second tribulation, which is the reign of the beast, but their chance of survival is the minutest of all the chances mortals have to survive in the battle. If the Eternity kingdom suffers violence and the violent takes it by force since the time of John the Baptist, according to what The Redeemer says in Matthew chapter eleven verse twelve, what is the chance of people surviving the two tribulation periods? If the condition of the mortals during first period of tribulation is as terrible as it is right now despite the fact that we have Comforter helping us in the battle with the use of the armour of war, what is the chance of survival of those who would be left on their own to go through the second tribulation period? During the second tribulation period, Comforter would no longer operate and the armour of war would not be effective at all. Mortals would be left to survive by their own strength, which we all know is not strength all. The Word says in First Samuel chapter two verse nine, "He (the Lord) will keep the feet of his saints, and the wicked shall be silent in darkness; for by strength shall no man prevail."

'The best chance of mortals to make it to Eternity kingdom is during this first period, not after The Redeemer has taken Believers away. Even during this first period of tribulation, the hope of mortals to get there lies in our hands. We have to ensure that no matter their conditions, they must stick to The Word, which is the map to Eternity kingdom. We on our part as warriors of The Redeemer must see to it that the enemies do not take the Lord from them, no matter what the enemies have taken away so far.

'I have one more thing to bring to your notice before I finally round up. We must understand that what is worth believing is worth dying for. The Redeemer says in Matthew chapter sixteen verse twenty-five, "for whoever save his life will lose it, but whoever loses his life for my sake will find it." Apart from the assurance of getting back our lives if we lose them, The Redeemer did the same for us by dying in our place when he came into this kingdom. We must be conscious of the fact that there are sacrifices we must make if we are really serious about helping others to get to Eternity kingdom. Failure to make the sacrifices can make us unworthy of the Lord just as my husband, giant Brethren tries to explain to us in the opening presentation.'

She pauses for a while before she concludes, 'I do hope we all understand what Comforter means when he says that he that has ears, let him hear what the Spirit says. Shall we rise on our feet for a discussion with The Redeemer who is waiting in The Spirit to hear our groaning and yearning?'

With sober reflection, all Believers rise on their feet for another round of serious discussion with The Redeemer.

CHAPTER TWENTY-TWO

'My lord,' Heresy says, going to Dragon who is having meeting with another batch of warriors in the level of Powers though not necessarily members of the rulers of darkness. They are actually getting information and instructions on how to help the rulers of darkness to further intensify their attacks against Believers.

Dragon looks startled as he asks, 'what's it, warrior?'

'Believers are getting more and more exposed to our secrets,' Heresy says, looking worried.

'So?' Dragon is indifferent.

'They causing me and my warriors lots of damages, my lord.'

Dragon gestures him to sit among the rest of the warriors.

Heresy sits almost at once.

'There is no cause for alarm,' Dragon says with confidence, looking round at them. 'You must understand a few things in the battle we are fighting against the mortals, including Believers. One of them is that they are blind and stupid. This is one of the reasons The Redeemer gives them Comforter to teach them virtually everything all Believers need know. Even if they read anything in The Word, they still need Comforter to interpret it to them. They are dumb, believe me. Whatever you hear them saying to one another can easily be wiped away by this warrior over here...' He gestures at a mild looking warrior.

The rest of the warriors look a little surprised. It is easy to know the question in their minds. 'Is he powerful enough to perform a job like that?'

'He is known by his deed just like everyone of you,' Dragon says. 'I raised him up when Believers are giving us problems.' He looks at the warrior and says, 'introduce yourself to your colleagues, warrior.'

He stands up slowly and says, 'my name is Forgetfulness.'

Heresy stands up and says, 'Forgetfulness is not enough to tackle Believers because they are always meditating on The Word

136

and learning many things at the Fellowship every time.'

'You're right, Heresy,' Dragon says and gestures at Indifference. 'The warrior over there is to contribute his part. If Indifference makes mortals unconcerned about whatever they have learnt, Forgetfulness can easily wipe out the knowledge or information from their memories.' He looks round at the warriors. 'I want you to get this information about the battle and the mortals before you ask me any question.

'First, you must understand that all mortals are weak; irrespective of whom they are. They have no strength of their own. Their brain capacities are not big enough to absorb enough vital information. The so-called geniuses among them are the most foolish among all mortals. What makes them more of zombies is the belief that they know so much. The more intelligent they are, the easier we can use them to serve our purposes. The more childish or foolish Believers seem to be, the more difficult it is for us to use them. The reason is that The Word mandates all Believers to be fools for the sake of The Redeemer.

'When dealing with those who lean on their understandings among the mortals, all we need to do before we can deceive and manipulate them is to package what they can perceive with their human senses and hide things of The Spirit from them. For instance, most of our inventions are perceived as scientific discoveries by mortal scientists.

'Now you know that mortals are weak, you must understand that their levels of weaknesses vary. What actually makes Believers stronger than one another is their determination to obey The Redeemer through The Word. The more they obey, the stronger they become. Although one of our warriors called Disobedience and his team are doing good job in causing the mortals to disobey The Word, everyone of you has the duty to make them kick against it through one way or the other. You must look for the weak areas of the mortals with particular focus on Believers. If we can get Believers to kick against The Word, they will never be effective in the battle against us. In fact, if we can take The Word from any of them, he is as good as dead.

'The next thing you must note in this battle is that you are not all trained to perform the same task. Thus you have different mortals you can tackle. For instance, I don't expect Heresy or Ignorance to go and tackle Believers who are well grounded in The Word. They would obviously fail, not because the warriors are weak but because they do not recognize their limits. To pave way for them to work, Apostasy

137

would need to work on such Believers...'

As Dragon educates his warriors, Believers continue to share information and knowledge of The Word at the conference.

Giant Faithful is the one addressing Believers at the conference. He says, '... one of our brothers who is now with The Redeemer called Martin Luther said and I quote, "I don't know what the future holds, but I know who holds the future."

'Trying to interpret the signs of the end time in line with The Word is one of the most difficult tasks for me but we thank the Lord for giant Brethren who laid a very solid foundation for us to build on. I'm counting on Comforter to make everyone understand reasons for the present events and what must be done.

'I have to talk about the evacuation of all Believers from the kingdom of man before the second tribulation just as our dearly beloved sister Hope tries to explain within the limited time she has.

'I don't want to use the word rapture because for one I am not an authority in teaching that part of the subject and, for two, the word; rapture is not really in The Word. Hence, if I use the word evacuation of Believers, I mean the movement of Believers from the kingdom of man to Eternity kingdom. By using this word: evacuation, I don't really mean rapture.

'Before I go further to explain evacuation of Believers, I want you to please turn with me to First Corinthians chapter fifteen verses fifty to fifty-four in The Word.' He waits for the people to open to the passage. 'The Word says, "Now this I say, brethren, that flesh and blood cannot inherit the kingdom of God; neither doth corruption inherit incorruption.

"Behold, I shew you a mystery; We shall not all sleep, but we shall all be changed,

"In a moment, in the twinkling of an eye, at the last trump: for the trumpet shall sound, and the dead shall be raised incorruptible, and we shall be changed.

"For this corruptible must put on incorruption, and this mortal must put on immortality.

"So when this corruptible shall have put on incorruption, and this mortal shall have put on immortality, then shall be brought to pass the saying that is written, Death is swallowed up in victory."

'The passages tell us many things,' Faithful continues after a brief pause. 'We are made to understand that flesh and blood which are characteristics of our mortal being cannot inherit the kingdom of The Father in Eternity. In other words, we can only dwell in kingdom of

138

man as mortals but we cannot go to Eternity kingdom with flesh and blood.

'The next passage tells us that what people call death is actually sleep if the person is a Believer. If the person is not a Believer, the book of Revelation chapter twenty-one verse eight calls it real death.

'Since we are talking as Believers, death is actually falling asleep and waking up in Eternity kingdom where another life begins.

'In verses fifty-one and fifty-two, we read of the mystery of this sleep. The Word tells us that we shall not all sleep, which means we shall not all die before the last trumpet is sounded. In the twinkling of an eye, the dead will be raised, and we shall be changed into incorruptible which immortal beings.' He pauses for a while before he continues. 'In the light of this, we need to consider the purposes of life in the kingdom of man as designed by The Father in Eternity.

'We have been giving wrong definition of life as a whole by various people and things. Some make us to see life as something we need to enjoy, even at the expense of others. Some things condition our minds to accept life as a rat race or a vicious circle, where we are born and breed. When we are old enough to learn, we would go to school where we are often times brainwashed by our brainwashed teachers. We go through a system or a structure that is designed as rat race. We are compelled sometimes by law to join the rat race, making it possible for brainwashed for people to decide our destinies through the use of politics and economy. We are given reasons we must be part of the system even though we do not agree with it. We join this rat race against our will, telling ourselves, "I have to go to school, get good grade, work hard to get enough money to take care of myself and family, get enough to invest into the future of my children so that they do not have to suffer..." The reasons for joining the rat race is endless. After spending the most productive part of our lives in this race, we become old and exhausted. Our family members we have spent the better part of our life begin to leave us one after the other, starting with the children who are old enough to join the rat race. After all the children are all gone, our spouses live us and we are left alone - in loneliness.

'Let ask you, my brothers and sisters, is this the way The Father in Eternity design our lives?'

Almost everybody replies, 'no!'

'You are talking as Believers,' Faithful says. 'If you ask the secular world or other Believers that are brainwashed, their answer would be different from ours. Why? The reason is that all mortals have

139

been given a wrong definition of life. As good as family is, we know better than to think that we are in the world to just raise families. We are not in the world to make money, which is the major incentive for joining the rat race. The Word tells us in Proverb chapter thirteen verse eleven, "Wealth gotten by vanity shall be diminished: but he that gathereth by labour shall increase."

'We can now say that the main purpose of life is not to make money, nor to raise family. The proof of this lies in the fact that none of these will follow us when we depart from this world.

'There are only two purposes of life as designed by The Father. The first purpose is to use life to serve the Lord. When I searched The Word for these words: serve the Lord, I found them in twenty-four places, which indicates the importance of serving the Lord. One the passages is found in Psalm chapter one hundred and two verse twenty-two. The Word says, "When the people are gathered together, and the kingdoms, to serve the LORD."

'The second purpose is that life is to be shared with others like our spouses, family members and other people around us by ministering to them in The Flesh, The Mind and The Spirit.

'When we use our lives for these purposes, we will enjoy it. The result of using life for selfish purpose is to lose it. The prove of that is found in the parable of The Redeemer in Luke chapter twelve verses sixteen to twenty-one. The Word says, "And he (the Lord) spake a parable unto them, saying, The ground of a certain rich man brought forth plentifully: And he thought within himself, saying, What shall I do, because I have no room where to bestow my fruits? And he said, This will I do: I will pull down my barns, and build greater; and there will I bestow all my fruits and my goods. And I will say to my soul, Soul, thou hast much goods laid up for many years; take thine ease, eat, drink, and be merry. But God said unto him, Thou fool, this night thy soul shall be required of thee: then whose shall those things be, which thou hast provided? So is he that layeth up treasure for himself, and is not rich toward God."

'Out of all The Father has given to this foolish man which include the gift of life, good health, power or wisdom to make money, the land where he sowed, the rain and the sunlight that made him to have so much harvest; God took only one which is the gift of life.

'Through The Word, we understand that Dragon not only gives mortals completely different purposes of life but also create vicious circle that keeps us engaged till we depart from the world. Our involvement in vicious circle or rat race makes it hard, if not impossible

140

for Believers to engage Dragon and his warriors in the battle that will determine the eternal destinations of other mortals.

'Giant Brethren said a lot that convinced everyone of us that we are truly guilty by omission to do what is right. We further need to understand that there are forces of the Dragon that are gathered against all mortals, especially Believers. Again, we thank the Lord for the leading presentation of giant Brethren who makes us to understand that we have been outnumbered. As if we don't have enough to contend with us, many Believers are engaged in rat race or vicious circle. Invariably, the race creates room for a deadly warrior of Dragon called Apostasy to operate. With the involvement of Apostasy and other deadly warriors, the battle is getting more and more intense. Going by all the signs we can read in The Word, we must expect things to get worse and the decisive battle to get more and more fierce. All these are just signs of the end of the first tribulation that indicate that the Lord will soon come for his own. As we have been taught, after the end of the first, all mortals must be prepared for the second and the great tribulation period.

'While giant Brethren was delivering the leading paper, I asked myself why I was born at this time when the battle is getting so severe that everybody is becoming vulnerable? I was able to get an answer through what he said. The answer is that we are alive at this time because we all given the privilege to be among the end time soldiers of The Redeemer. Going by his presentation, I realized that my question was born out of selfish interest. We are all truly guilty of selfishness. I will define selfishness as lack of considerations or feelings for others. If we are not selfish, why are we not reaching out to other mortals who we know are heading to Doom kingdom? Why do Believers have to wait for Dragon to take the battle into the political, economic and social structures; knowing fully well that mortals will damn the eternal consequences? Well, we know Dragon rules the world but Believers can make it ungovernable for him and dictate to the affairs of mortals in The Spirit. After all it is in The Spirit we can get victories for ourselves and for others. If we are not selfish, why didn't we sacrifice our personal comfort or conveniences just to avert the destructions of countless number of mortals that are already in Doom? I put it to myself and to everyone here that any Believer that is comfortable at this time of tribulation is guilty of selfishness. This may sound harsh but let us see the basis for this in James chapter four verse seventeen in The Word. The Word says, "therefore, to him who knows to do good and does not do it, to him it is sin." Here we see that

141

doing the wrong thing can be by commission or omission. Most the offences of Believers in the class of matured ones or giants are always in omissions to do things that are right. A mortal called Edmund Burke said that the only thing necessary for the triumph of evil is for good men to do nothing. So if there are mortals responsible for the pathetic condition of kingdom of man today, they are called Believers.

'We have sacrificed precious mortals while running rat race and the shut our conscience up by giving ourselves reasons for joining the race. Believers now dine with their enemies at the expense of their eternal life and the lives of other mortals. We have neglected our primary assignment which is to serve the Lord and minister to others. Believers who are the hope of other mortals are now in the position that is created by Apostasy. This position, which we can call the age of Apostasy is the time The Redeemer talked about in Luke chapter eighteen verse eight where he asked if he will find us faithful when he comes to evacuate all Believers.

'Let us consider the first set of signs of the end time as foretold in The Word by The Redeemer in Matthew chapter twenty-four verse four to fourteen. The Redeemer tells us in that passage that we must be careful not to be deceived by anyone or anything. We have seen and heard of cases of destructive lies everywhere. We have witnessed at least two different wars that shed blood of millions of mortals in all areas of the kingdom of man. This is not to talk of civil wars and civil unrest that are claiming other millions of lives . We've witnessed kingdoms rising against kingdoms, famines upon famines like what the people call global economic crisis. We have heard of earthquakes at various places. We have witnessed the dark age when Believers are being tortured and made to go and rest because they refuse to deny the Lord. There are so many false Believers who are mortal warriors of Dragon though they do not know they are serving their arch-enemy - Dragon. These armies are fond of undoing what the few soldiers of The Redeemer are doing.

'Now is really the age of Apostasy when the first love Believers have for The Redeemer is growing cold. It is the time Dragon is striking the hardest blow against us, trying to destroy hope of mortals.

'The age of apostasy is much more dangerous than the age of persecution of early Believers. You will understand why I would have preferred to be born at the time of early Believers who were far stronger than that of the modern days.

'Part of the jobs of Apostasy is to condition our minds to accept things that are not acceptable to The Redeemer, make our love for him grow cold, kill our zeal in the battle and silence our cries on to The Father as we say, "Abba Father!"

'I want to assure you of one thing: we shall get victory if we don't give up. We shall get victory if we don't compromise our stand with The Redeemer. We shall get victory if we don't negociate with the enemies. We shall get victory if we don't defile ourselves with the food that is prepared by mortal servants of our immortal enemies! We must say to ourselves: "This is a battle to the finish! No retreat, no surrender!" No matter our conditions, we shall fight this battle! We shall fight even without food in our stomachs. We shall fight in perils! We shall die fighting the enemies of mortals! Our enemies know we are determined to push them back away from other mortals for this battle is one of the major purposes of our lives. They want to engage us in The Flesh and in The Mind. I have bad news for these immortal enemies. We shall not fight them in The Flesh because it can cause the casualties of mortals! We shall not fight in The Mind because the battle there can cause insanities! But we shall fight them in The Spirit because, according the second Corinthians chapter ten verse four and five, our weapons of our warfare are not carnal, but mighty through God to the pulling down of strong holds, casting down imaginations, and every high thing that exalts itself against the knowledge of God, and bringing into captivity every thought to the obedience of Christ...!'

There is a standing ovation as all Believers, including Faith, Faithful's wife feel charged with The Word. After a while, they sit down again.

Faith feels so joyful and excited that tears of joy run down her eyes. She feels very happy that her dream and the prophesy of Gentle that she would marry a giant had come to pass at last.

'Apostasy is good at making Believers to be indifferent in spite of evidences of things not yet seen,' Faithful continues. 'For instance, if someone comes to tell us that our enemies are bringing war into this hall, some may be moved while some may not. If perhaps the enemies do not come on time, some of those who believed that war is actually coming may lose their convictions. That state of losing conviction is the work of Apostasy.

'Believers know that The Redeemer is coming like a thief in the night, according to Second Peter chapter three verse ten, but many of us are not really prepared to meet the Lord. Some are prepared but they are not preparing others. Everyone of us, especially those who are listening to me now has a duty to prepare others for Eternity

143

kingdom. Going by the activities of both Believers and other people, more than ninety percent of all of us in the kingdom of man may not get to Eternity kingdom. The Redeemer cannot afford to lose all these people.

'As we gather here to discuss about expanding Eternity kingdom by reaching out to other people, Dragon and his warriors are also having constant meetings on how to reduce number of people of The Redeemer. If there is anything that would really accomplish this great task of reaching out to the people, it is for every Believer to be involved in the wok of The Redeemer. If we are all doing all we can to reach out, we'll be having more soldiers in the army of The Redeemer. The more soldiers we have, the lesser the work.

'Every Believer has what it takes to terrorize our immortal enemies and reach out to other mortals. No matter who you are or what your age; gender, status is, you must be much involved in reaching out. Because the Dragon is determined to keep as many people as possible in his army, he and his warriors will try to use vicious circle and rat race to ensnare us. He and his warriors will engage us in the battle when we are on this quest. Matured Believers and giants will face more attack than babes but the good news is, according to The Word in First Samuel chapter seventeen verse forty-seven, the battle is the Lord's. In that passage, we see that The Redeemer does not save with things we can see.

'We've got the power of The Redeemer to pull down anything that holds us down. We can put the warriors and all the combined forces of Dragon into a flight if we come together as one! The Word makes us to understand in Deuteronomy chapter thirty-two verse thirty that one of us can chase a thousand at a time but two can put ten thousand to flight if they fight their enemies together. You can imagine the disaster we can create for Dragon if all of us in this hall alone come together to fight him and his armies. Dragon knows much more about the strengths of Believers than any of us. So he uses Disunity to divide and rule us. A lot of us are more concerned about our denominational doctrines. We focus on the flaws of our leaders and so many little things we do not need in the battle. We have to put an end to our differences and dwell on common ground which is The Word! It doesn't matter how fierce the battle, if we keep our sanity in The Word, we will survive in the battle, however fierce!'

Faithful pauses for a while. There is complete silence as the rest expect more from him. Unable to control himself, he falls on his kneels and begins to cry. Most of listeners are puzzled. He says within his sobs. 'I wish every Believer knows that we cannot survive in this battle without one another. If any of us fight this battle alone, he will not last before he is brought down. The reason is that we've been outnumbered and surrounded by enemies within and without. So many of the Lord's soldiers have decamped to the camp of Dragon.' He stands up slowly. 'Let's cry to The Redeemer now to help us fight this battle and send more soldiers into out midst. Also, we must ask for Spirit of unity among Believers.'

Within few minutes Believers are on their feet again, crying loud to The Redeemer to deliver every mortal in the world.

THE END

CHECK OUT OTHER BOOKS BY DIPO TOBY ALAKIJA

Each Serves Either As Edifying Or Evangelical Or Missionary Or Academic Tool At Home, School, Bible Clubs, Sunday Schools, Church, Office And Other Fellowships

THE BATTLE OF THE CONQUERORS
ISBN: 978-49874-7-3 ISBN: ISBN: 978-978-49874-0-7-9

Wickedness takes over the land of Bondage from First Couple and subjects everybody into slavery without giving anybody the chance to be free. Love brings The Redeemer from Eternity and offers the slaves the chance to escape. Wickedness soon declares war and engages everyone in the battle. The Redeemer makes the redeemed people Conquerors by giving them the armour of war and Comforter but Wickedness cannot be undone. He has several thousands of years of experience in the war. So he is quick to recognize the weakness of the redeemed people who are ignorant of their strengths and advantages. Although the Conquerors fight like immutable giants, rescuing victims of war, many people suffer heavy casualties.

Since King Wickedness knows that a redeemed person is strong enough to chase one thousand of his warriors at a time, and two would put ten thousand into flight, he enlists as one of his warriors the people's deadliest enemy called Disunity.

Wickedness is able to strike the people by making them to fight with one another, turning what is supposed to be their best moments in the battle into tales of woes.

NO MORE TEARS TO SHED
ISBN: 978-49874-3-0 ISBN: 978-978-74-3-1

Kidnappers took Tokunbo away from his grand parents in a city in Nigeria when he was a little boy. A nice woman found him in another town and gave him a false identity. She spoilt him with love, making him to grow into a rebellious teenager that was not appreciated anywhere. When Janet made him a Christian, however, life began to make sense to him until the day he was beaten to the point of death for the offence he knew nothing about. He left the town for the city which, unknown to him, held his true identity and the link to his parents in the United States. To find them was only a question of time.

FOOTSTEPS IN THE MUD

ISBN: 978-36348-9-5 ISBN: 978-978-36348-9-3

The Drama Package Of Results Of Research Works That trace Global And Societal Vices To The Corrupt Or Lost Of Family Values

The 13-Episode drama book involves Bosede who learnt many wrong things from her parents' conduct and foul language. She was forced to marry Kola when she became pregnant. Using her mother's method to handle her father, she tried to subject Kola to her control. In the course of that, she made life terrible for him. Although her mother tried to warn her of the implications of maltreating her husband but Bosede has grown out of control. Consequently, while looking for peace, Kola was pushed out of the house. He made friends with some guys who taught him the unholy ways of life and influenced him to become a menace in the house.

Junior who was born at time the couple never proved to be responsible parents also learnt wrong things from them. He decided to follow his father's footsteps by taking alcohol when he was in primary school. As if that was not bad enough, he tried to teach other children in the school the madness in his home. A school teacher, however, was able to influence him and his mother by teaching them Christian morals. Even then, Junior was soon caught in the crossfire at home as his father tried to enlist him as a future member of a secret cult that posed as a social club.

SUCCESSFUL CHRISTIANITY AND BASIC MINISTRIES

ISBN: 978-49874-6-0

A Collection Of Resource Materials That Precedes Christian Ministries And Basic Leadership Course Book

The first question is how Christianity is practiced even in a hostile environment. Next to that is the question about the potentials of Christians in spite of their apparent limitations. The other issues are connected to the successes, deliverance, callings, basic ministries of all Christians and evangelism. Various schools of thoughts have attempted these questions but many answers only portray Christianity as a form of religion instead of a way of life as specified by God. Some answers give room for compromise, hypocrisies, dogmas and denominational doctrines. The misconceptions about these areas of Christianity have brought about worldliness instead of righteousness and false achievements instead of fulfillment.

This book which contains six different subjects had been used to hold seminars at various levels, train ministers and Christian workers in Bible Schools and to equip the Church. It explains in simple terms the seemingly complex issues on practice of Christianity, Potentials, Deliverance, God's Kind Of Success, Evangelism and Basic Ministries of a Christian with Biblical principles, life transforming stories and illustrations.

CHRISTIAN COMMUNICATIONS AND HUMAN RESOURCE COURSE BOOK
ISBN: 978-073-509-7 ISBN: 978-978-073-509-8

The world is not in need of those who will fix errors of humanity but in dire need of matured Christians that would use their gifts to communicate the word of God and lead their families, the Church, communities and their countries in the way of righteousness. Very few of them, however, seem to have what it takes to take their positions as leaders and ministers in their spheres despite their God-given potentials. Thus this Course Book - a compilation of six resource materials on Christian Oral Communications, Christian Written Communications, Christian  Drama Communications, Christian Musical Communications, Christian Human Resources and Children Evangelism - makes serious attempts to introduce everybody into various creative ministries that are required in the Body of Christ and in the world. It teaches in a simple manner the management of human resources and the ways Christians can use their gifts to reach out to souls through speaking, writing, drama, media, musical and children ministries. The resource materials equip and help individuals to identify their callings, providing Biblical principles and guidelines on how to be effective and productive in the service of the Lord in spite of the hostile environments.

CHRISTIAN MINISTRIES AND BASIC LEADERSHIP
ISBN: 978-36348-7-9 ISBN: 978-978-36348-7-9

A Collection Of Resource Materials That Follows Up Successful Christianity And Basic Ministries Course Book

As it is common to say that the hood does not make a monk, the dignified positions and bogus titles of many Christian leaders in modern days do not really make them Gospel Ministers.

This course book - a compilation of five resource materials on Missions And Outreach Ministries, Christian Communication Arts, Christian Leadership,

148

Christian Education Methodology and Ministries Of Improvisations - aims at making every matured Christian an effective minister and leader at their respective homes, communities and nations. It teaches various ways Christians can communicate the word of God, meeting up to their responsibilities as ministers and leaders that reconcile people to God, edifying the Body Of Christ and reaching out to souls at the same time.

All of the resource materials are in use in Bible Schools like College Of Christian Education And Missions, in Churches and other ministries to raise Christian workers, Evangelists, Missionaries and other Ministers that serve at various levels and leadership capacities.

INSANITY OF HUMANITY
ISBN: 978-36348-6-0 ISBN: 978-978-36348-6-2
The Results Of Research Works Into Various Methods Of Brainwashing

Man is made to exercise his freewill. The mind of his own and the power to choose between right and wrong, good and evil, light and darkness is about to be washed away through brainwashing. The agents of control dubbed as Secret Government by John Todd (the top Illuninati defector) have put necessary machinery in place to ensure that all human beings are in conformity in their thinking and ways of life, trying to wipe away diversity, which makes each person unique.

This book attempts to shed light on how the techniques of mind control are applied through the use of propaganda, education, entertainments, drugs, religions, media and other means of communications. It is the result of research works, some of which are based on findings of various researchers and writers like Bugger Lugz, Edward Hunter, Hadley Cantril, Herbert Krugman, David L. Robb, Vaughan Bell, Juliana Gomez, Ryan Duffy Vice, Henry Makow, David Nicholls, Fritz Springmeire, Steven Hassan, Renate Thienel, Debra Pursell, Mary Pride and a host of others who are acknowledged in this book.

THE UNROMANTIC LOVE BIRDS
ISBN: 978-4987-5-7 ISBN: 978-978-4974-5-5
And other short stories about love and marriages

They were very much in love right from their school days but when they got married and had children, romance became the game Charles' wife refused to play. No matter how much he tried to make her understand the unbearable condition her unromantic attitude has subjected him into, she would not change. Consequently, after enduring for so long, he was forced to look for the women that would make up for her weakness. He unofficially married a beautiful lady of insane jealousy. Though she was ready to give him what was missing in his marriage, it soon dawn on him that he has solved one big problem only to create a bigger one.

NETWORK BIBLE CLUB
YOUTH AND ADULT BOOK ONE
ISBN: 978 - 978- 49874-9-X ISBN: 978-978-49874-9-3

A collection of 26 life transforming stories, 26 poems, 26 hymn tuned songs and weekly Bible lessons

The issue of moral instructions in schools and at homes is threatened with extinction. Consequently, so many youths are involved in prostitution, drug addictions, cultism, fraudulent practices, armed robberies and other crimes. Those who are supposed to be trained as leaders in various walks of life are the ones posing serious threats to many lives. Many parents who fail to add moral values to the upbringing of their children often times breed potential criminals under their roofs without knowing it. Apart from these, many other people negatively influence young ones through the media, music, publications, films, conduct and foul language; making them to lose their moral and family values.

This book one just like the rest of other volumes is an attempt to bring back moral instructions into schools and campuses through the use of stories, hymn tuned songs, poems, Bible lessons and class activities. It is designed to assist teachers and ministers in Secondary Schools, Bible Clubs, Churches and Campus Fellowships to teach people, especially youths the Word of God and serves as a school text book in subjects relating to literature, music and other creative works.

FOUNDATION BIBLE CLUB A-Z STORY BOOK
ISBN: 978-49874-2-2 ISBN: 978-978-49874-2-4

Volume 1 With 26 Stories, 26 Bible Lessons, 26 Rhymes And 26 Songs For Book For Young Minds

An adage says, "a man who builds a house without building his child builds what the child will later sell." Proverbs 22:6 says, "train up a child in the way he should go: and when he is old, he will not depart from it." This book is an attempt to assist parents and teachers to meet up to the challenges that befall them in carrying out this important function in the light of the moral decadence that is prevailing all over the world.

150

The first edition of the book was used by several thousands of teachers, ministers and parents in schools, Churches and homes to build the moral values of young ones. Apart from the stories, songs and Bible passages for the young ones to study, there is a seminar material that is based on the lecture which the author delivered to school proprietors, children ministers and Christian professionals in this volume.

RANSOM FOR LOVE
ISBN: 978-49874-8-1 ISBN: 978-978-4987-4-8-6

She accepted his marriage proposal without knowing the kind of person he was. She soon discovered that he was a mean and ruthless guy who was always ready to get whatever he wanted by all means even if he has to pay for it with the lives of others. She was in his bondage, especially when her parents who believed he was a generous and gentleman were on his side.

Because she considered the proposal to marry him as a marriage engagement with the devil incarnate, she decided that she would rather die than to share her life with him. Then out of the blues, this passionate gentleman sneaked into her life despite all she did to discourage him. She could not resist his love for her when he offered to set her free from the devil incarnate. Then the battle began – sooner than they anticipated.

THE WEIGHT OF DEATH
ISBN: 9978-36348-0-1 ISBN: 978-978-36348-0-0
(Story Of The Spirit Eyes Series)

PLAY ONE: HORROR IN THE FAMILY: Talimi probably did not envisage his death when he was trying to compel his son, Damola to succeed him in the occult Brotherhood. Other members of the secret cult were aware of the battle between them. So when Talimi died; his family, especially Damola who was a diehard Christian began to fall prey to the cult. Using all their powers and the spirit that posed as Talimi's ghost, the cult waged war against the family, tormenting and making them to be at loggerheads.

PLAY TWO: RITUAL KIDS' KIDNAPPERS: Victor and the rest of the members of the School Bible Club were taught that there are lots of evil people in this world but he did not understand why God allowed him to be among the children that were taken away from their parents. He soon understood that he was to be used by God to rescue other children who did not know that everyone that truly believes in Jesus has the power to overcome evil.

PLAY THREE: THE WEIGHT OF DEATH: Awoseun would not have known the real source of problems of mankind if his father had not given him the power to see demons tormenting the people in different ways. What he was yet to know, however, was the power of light over darkness. When he was caught in crossfire between these powers, he desperately sought for deliverance.

CALVARY ROCK RESOURCE BOOKLETS
ISSN: 1595 93X

The Quarterly Missionary Booklets That Are Designed To Teach Children, Youths And Adults In Schools, Fellowships, Churches, At Homes, Office And Other Places.

Although all the various volumes of this booklet can be used independently of other books but it is recommended that it should be used as part of supplementary materials to make up for Foundation and Network Bible Club Story Books for both children and adults in School, Church, Campus, Office and other Fellowships.

Each of the volume is rich with quarterly Bible lessons, stories, drama, songs, seminar, tract materials and a host of other things that can be used to edify, educate, entertains and evangelize every category of people, ranging from children to elderly persons.

Every volume is designed to equip school teachers, ministers in Churches or campus or office fellowships and other people who wish to work with the Lord.

All These And Other Books Are Distributed Worldwide And Published By The Publishing House Of Calvary Rock Resources
*Ikenne-Remo, Nigeria
*Manchester, United Kingdom
*New York, United States

www.calvaryrock.org